# Hieroglyphic Dictionary

## A Middle Egyptian Vocabulary

compiled by

**Bill Petty, PhD**

Museum Tours Press
Littleton, Colorado

Published by

**Museum Tours Press**
**A division of**
**Museum Tours, Inc.**
**7110 Old farm Road**
**Littleton, CO 80128**

www.museum-tours.com



ISBN - 978-1-48127-165-3

Cover Image: From the Annals of Thutmose III in Karnak
Photo by Bill Petty

Printed in the United States of America, 2013
13-1

# Introduction

This paperback Hieroglyphic Dictionary has been created to fill a need for an inexpensive dictionary that is relatively comprehensive. Words included are primarily taken from monumental inscriptions, of the type one is most likely to encounter in Egypt or in museums. At under 200 pages it cannot be all inclusive. However it is hoped that the choice of words included meets the needs of students and others who want a book that is easily carried, yet relatively thorough.

The organization is fairly standard. Words are listed in alphabetical order, using the standard phonetic alphabet (printed in bold italic). When the hieroglyphic spelling of a word does not match the actual transliteration, the Hieroglyphic spelling takes precedence in the listing. Thus 𓐍𓏏𓆑, which is actually transliterated as ***ẖft***, is listed under ***ẖt*** (as well as under ***ẖf***). In those rare cases where an obscure determinative is used, it will sometimes be replaced with a similar sign or by a simple crosshatch pattern,

In addition to the authors own observations, much is owed to the following for the contents of this work: E. Wallis Budge, Mark Collier, Raymond Faulkner, Alan Gardiner, Bill Manley, Kurt Sethe, Karl-Theodor Zauzich

This book is the result of several years of research and work. I want to thank my wife, Nancy, for putting up with the inconvenience.

Comments, suggestions or corrections are always welcome. Please send them to mt@museumotours.com, with the subject line "Hieroglyphic Dictionary".

# Contents
## with some common signs used to begin words

Introduction     3

| | | |
|---|---|---|
| ꜣ | | 7 |
| i | | 11 |
| y | | 28 |
| ꜥ | | 29 |
| w | | 38 |
| b | | 50 |
| p | | 55 |
| f | | 60 |
| m | | 61 |
| n | | 75 |
| r | | 87 |
| h | | 94 |

| | |
|---|---|
| *ḥ* | 97 |
| *ḫ* | 112 |
| *ẖ* | 121 |
| *s* | 125 |
| *š* | 150 |
| *ḳ* | 158 |
| *k* | 162 |
| *g* | 165 |
| *t* | 168 |
| *ṯ* | 174 |
| *d* | 178 |
| *ḏ* | 183 |

**ꜣ** — *ꜣ* vulture

**ꜣꜣ** — *ꜣꜣ* ruin(s)

*ꜣꜣtꜣ* Nubian chieftain(?) or his name(?)

**ꜣy** — *ꜣyt* to pale, blanch

**ꜣꜥ** — *ꜣꜥbt* opression

**ꜣw** — *ꜣw* length, long, joyful, pleasing

*ꜣw* death, deceased (lit - stretched out)

*ꜣwi͗* be long, stretch out, expanded, joyful

*ꜣwi͗, ꜣwy* extend, announce, arouse, present (an offering)

*ꜣw ḥr* farsighted

*ꜣwt* length (of time)

*ꜣwt* long knife

*ꜣwt i͗b* joy, happiness (lit -wide heart)

*ꜣw ḏrt* generous (lit - extend a hand)

*r ꜣw f* entire, all

*sꜣwi͗* lengthen, prolong

*sꜣwy ḥr* keep an eye on

*sꜣwi͗-i͗b* to gladden (lit - to lengthen the heart)

*ꜣwḥ* do violence

*ꜣwt, ꜣwt ꜥ* gifts, offerings

**ꜣb** — *ꜣb* stop, cease, stay, tarry, avoid

*ꜣbw* cessation

*sꜣb* cause to delay

*ꜣbi͗* to desire, wish

*ꜣbꜣb* be delighted

*ꜣb n* has desired

*ꜣby* panther, leopard

*ꜣbw* to brand, scorch

*ꜣbw* elephant

*ꜣbw* ivory

*ꜣbw* Elephantine Island (UE)

*ꜣbḫ [m]* unite, join, mix, engage [with]

*ꜣbḫ [m]* mingle [with]

*ꜣbt* family, relatives

*ꜣbd* month

*ꜣbḏw* Abydos (UE)

**ꜣp** *ꜣpd* bird, goose, duck, fowl

*ꜣpd* rush forward

*ipdw* furniture

**ꜣf** *ꜣfꜥ* greed, be greedy

**ꜣm** *ꜣm* burn

*sꜣm* cause to burn, burn up

*ꜣmi [ḥr]* mix, compound [with]

*ꜣmm* seize, grip, grasp, attack

*ꜣmmt* grasp

*ꜣms* club, mace, royal scepter, staff, wield (an "**ames**")

*ꜣms* show solicitude

*ꜣms* lie, falsehood

**ꜣr** *ꜣr [ḥr]* restrain, hold back [from], drive away, oppress

**ꜣh** *ꜣhw* pain, trouble, misery

*ꜣhw* sufferer

*ꜣhmt* sorrow

*ꜣhd* be feeble, faint

ꜣḥ *ꜣḥt* field, arable land, earth

ꜣḫ *ꜣḫ* papyrus thicket

*ꜣḫ* spirit, spirit like nature

*ꜣḫ* be glorious, beneficial, useful

*ꜣḫw* power

*ꜣḫt* what is good, useful, beneficial

*sꜣḫ* beatify, make blessed

*sꜣḫw* glorifications, beatific spells

*ꜣḫꜣḫ* (ship's) spars

*ꜣḫw* sunshine

*ꜣḫ-bit* Chemmis (North Delta)

*ꜣḫt* inundation (season)

*ꜣḫt* uraeus

*ꜣḫt* arable land

*ꜣḫt* flame

*ꜣḫt* god's eye, eye of Ra

*ꜣḫt* horizon

*ꜣḫt* horizon, tomb

*ꜣḫty* of the horizon (dweller)

*ꜣḫty* of a remote people

ꜣẖ *ꜣẖꜥ* to scratch, scrape, carve, engrave

*ꜣẖꜥt* scratch, scar

ꜣs *ꜣs* soft inner body parts

*ꜣs* to hasten, to overtake, quickly, hurry, flow fast

 ***ꜣsb*** fierce, glowing

 ***ꜣsḫ*** reap

 ***ꜣst*** (goddess) Isis

***ꜣš***  ***ꜣšr*** to roast

 ***ꜣšrt*** roasted meat

***ꜣḳ***  ***ꜣḳ*** perish

 ***ꜣḳw*** ruin, misfortune

 ***ꜣḳḥw*** axe

***ꜣk***  ***ꜣkr*** (earth god) Aker

***ꜣt***  ***ꜣt*** attack, striking power

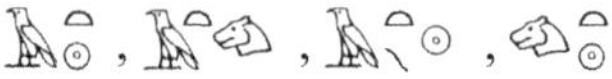 ***ꜣt*** instant, moment

 ***ꜣtp [m]*** to load [with]

 ***ꜣtpw*** load

 ***ꜣtf*** "**atef**" crown

 ***ꜣtf*** be crowned

***ꜣṯ***  ***ꜣṯp [m]*** to load [with]

 ***ꜣṯpw*** load, cargo

***ꜣd***  ***ꜣd*** be aggressive, be angry, be savage, attack, anger

 ***ꜣḏw*** agressor

**ỉ**

*ỉ* I, me, my

*ỉ* I, me, my (fem)

*ỉ* I, me, my (god or king)

*ỉ* "O"

*ỉ* to say

*ỉ* reed

**ỉꜣ**

*ỉꜣt* stick, rod

*ỉꜣꜥ* skirt

*ỉꜣw* praise

*ỉꜣwỉ* be old, attain old age

*ỉꜣ(y)t* old woman

*ỉꜣw* old man

*ỉꜣwt* old age

*ỉꜣby* left hand (east) side

*ỉꜣb* east wind

*ỉꜣbt* the east

*ỉꜣbty* east, eastern

*ỉꜣbtyw* Easterners

*ỉꜣbtyw* the east of

*ỉꜣbtt* the East

*ỉꜣbtt* snare

*ỉꜣm* tree (general)

*ỉꜣm* be gracious, charming

*ỉꜣmt* graciousness, charm, kindliness, favor

*ỉꜣmw* splendor, brilliance

*ỉꜣm(w)* tent

***ỉꜣrw*** reeds

***ỉꜣrrt*** vine

***ỉꜣrrt*** grapes

***ỉꜣḫi*** be inundated

***ỉꜣs*** bald

***ỉꜣš*** call

***ỉꜣḳ*** to leap

***ỉꜣḳt*** leeks

***i(ꜣ)kb*** mourn

***ỉꜣt*** back

***ỉꜣt*** mound

***ỉꜣꜣ*** ruins

***ỉꜣt*** ruins

***ỉꜣt*** standard, banner

***ỉꜣt*** office, rank, function

***ỉꜣtyw*** office holder

***ỉꜣt*** be mutilated, missing

***siꜣt*** purloin, cheat

***siꜣty*** cheat

***ỉꜣtt*** milk, cream

***ỉꜣṯ*** be mutilated, injured, missing (see also ***ỉꜣt***)

***ỉꜣṯw*** shambles

***ỉꜣṯw*** place of execution

***idw*** pestilence

***ỉꜣdt*** dew, pouring rain (see also ***idt***)

***ỉꜣdt*** net

***ii*** ***ii*** come, welcome!

*ii-wy* how welcome (is), welcome!

*iy* — *iyt* mishap, harm

*iꜥ* — *iꜥ* ascend, arise

*iꜥꜣ* skirt

*iꜥi* wash, cleanse

*iꜥi ib* satisfy (one's) desire, appetite, wrath (lit - cleanse the heart)

*iꜥb* cup

*iꜥb* unite

*(i)ꜥbt ẖꜣt* burial (lit - uniting the corpse)

*m ꜥb* together with, in the company of

*iꜥn* baboon, sacred baboon

*iꜥnw* lamentation, sorrow, woe

*iꜥr* ascend, mount, approach

*sꜥr* make to ascend, offer up

*iꜥrt* uraeus

*iꜥḥ* moon

*iw* — *iw* indeed, verily, in fact, it happed that, (etc) (a part of the verb “to be“ but implies fact, difficult to translate and is sometimes omitted in translation)

*iw ms* Indeed not!

*iw* come

*iw f ꜥꜣ f* one who rises in rank

*iw* island

*iw* dog

*iw* wrong, crime

*iw* complaint

*siw [r]* bring a complaint [against]

*i̓w(y)* one without a boat

*i̓wyt* wrongdoing

*i̓wyt* sanctuary, house, quarter (of city)

*i̓wꜣ* ox

*i̓wꜣ* beef

*i̓wyt* street, house, area, sanctuary

*i̓wnyt* hall of columns

*i̓wꜥ* thigh (of beef), femur

*i̓wꜥ* inherit, inherit from

, *i̓wꜥ [m]* reward [with]

, , , *i̓wꜥw* heir

*i̓wꜥt* heiress

, , , , *i̓wꜥt* heritage, inheritance

, *i̓wꜥyt* garrison, soldiery, troops

*i̓wꜥw* ring

*i̓wf* meat, flesh

*i̓w ms* mistatement

*i̓wn* complexion, nature, color

*i̓wn* column, pillar

*i̓wnyt* hall of columns

, *i̓wny* Armant (Hermonthis) (UE)

*i̓wnyt* Esna (Latopolis) (UE)

, *i̓wnw* Heliopolis (ancient On) (LE)

, *i̓wnw šmꜥw* Thebes (lit - Heliopolis of Upper Egypt)

*i̓wnn* sanctuary

*i̓w-nsrsr* a mythical locality

*ỉwnt* bow

*ỉwn(ty) sty* Nubian bowman

*ỉwntyw* tribesmen, nomads

*ỉwntyw styw* Nubian bowmen

*ỉwnt* Dendera (UE)

*ỉwr* conceive, become pregnant

*ỉwh [m][ḥr]* to load [with]

*ỉwḥ* to moisten, water, irrigate

*ỉwḥw* inundation

*ỉwsw* balance, scale

*ỉ(w)grt* necropolis

*(ỉw)t(y)(ỉ)* which ... not, who ... not

*ỉwtyw* corruption

*ỉwtn* ground, floor

*ỉwd* to separate

*r-ỉwd ... r* between ... and

*ỉwdt* separation

*ỉb* — *ỉb* suppose, imagine

*ỉb* kid

*ỉb* wish

*ỉb* heart, seat of intelligence

*ꜣwt ỉb* joy, happiness (lit -wide heart)

*ỉꜥỉ ỉb* satisfy (one's) desire, appetite, wrath (lit - cleanse the heart)

*ỉms ỉb* pleasant, kindly disposed (to)

*ꜥm ỉb* to faint, lose consciousness

*ꜥm ỉb ḥr* be thoughtless, neglectful

***ꜥḥꜥ ib*** persistent

***wꜣḥ-ib*** patient, well disposed

***wbꜣ ib*** intelligent, capable, inlightened

***wmt-ib*** stout hearted

***wḥꜥ ib*** capable, skilled

***mr ib n*** be sorry for

***mr ḥr ib n*** be displeasing to

***mḥ-ib*** be trustworthy, trusted

***mtt n ib*** rectitude, affection

***m mtt nt ib-f*** following his heart

***nḏm ib*** joyful

***rḳ ib*** disaffected one, rebel

***rdi ib m-sꜣ*** be anxious about

***rdi ib ḫnt*** pay attention to

***ḥꜣt ib*** grief, sadness

***[m] ḥr(y)-ib*** [in] the midst of

***ḥr(y)-ib(y)*** who dwells in (said of deities)

***ẖrt-ib*** wish, desire

***ḫꜣkw-ib*** disaffected, rebel

***sꜣwi-ib*** to gladden (lit - to lengthen the heart)

***snk-ib*** haughtiness

***sḫmḫ ib*** recreation, sport

***st-ib*** affection (lit - place in the heart)

***kfꜣ-ib*** be discreet, trustworthy, careful

***kfꜣ-ib [ḥr]*** trustworthy [in]

***ṯꜣ-ib*** able

***di m ib-f*** determine

***dns ib*** reluctant (lit - heavy heart)

***ib(ꜣ)*** to dance

***ibꜣ*** dance

***ibꜣ(w)*** dances

***ibꜣ*** draughsman

***ibi*** be thirsty

***ibt*** thirst

***ibw*** refuge

***ibwy*** halliards ( of boat)

***ib(ꜣ)r*** stallion

***ibḥ*** tooth, tusk

***ibḥ*** priest who performs libations

***ibḥw*** one who performs libations

***ibs*** a king's headress

*ip* ***ip*** to count, calculate, reckon, access, pay, examine, heed, assemble

***ipt*** reckoning, census

***ip ḏt. f*** grow up (id) (lit - count his self)

***sip*** revise, inspect, assign, examine, destine, organize

***sipty*** revision, inspect, investigation

***ipw*** that

***ipw*** payments

***ipwty*** messenger

***ipn*** this

***ipt*** harim, private apartments

***ipt nsw*** king's harim

***ipt*** measure of 4 **"hekat"** (~18 liters)

***ipt*** mission, message, occupation

*ipwty* messenger

*ipt* festival of the 12th month

*iptw* that

*iptn* this

*ipt-swt* (the temple of) Karnak

*ipdw* furniture

*ip ḏt. f* grow up (id) (lit - count his self)

*if* — *ifd* flee

*ifd* quadruple

*ifdt* four of, quartet

*ifdy* square of cloth

*im* — *im* there, therein, therewith

*im* in, as, by, with, from, together with

*im* a body part, form, shape

*imw* certain body parts

*im(ꜣ)* tree (general)

*imꜣ* be gracious, charming, kind, gentle, pleasing

*imꜣt* graciousness, charm,

*simꜣ* make well disposed kindliness, favor

*im(ꜣ)w* splendor, brilliance

*im(ꜣ)(w)* tent

*imꜣḫ* spinal cord

*imꜣḫ* venerated state, revered, honored

*imi* to mourn

*imi* not be (negation)

*imi* to give, place, cause, grant

***ỉmy*** mine, yours

***ỉmy*** who (which) is in, being in

***ỉmy ỉb*** favorite

***ỉmy ỉs*** councillor

***ỉmy wrt*** west side, starboard

***ỉmyw-ḥꜣt*** those of former times, ancestors

***ỉmy bꜣḥ*** who is in the presence, who existed before time, ancestor

***ỉmy rn f*** list of names

***ỉmy ḥꜣt*** prototype, example, pattern, who (which) is in front

***ỉmy ḫnt*** priestly title

***ỉmy ḫt*** who follows, accompanies, bodyguard, attendant, posterity

***ỉmy-sꜣ*** attendant, bodyguard

***ỉmy st*** acolyte, helper

***(m) (r) ỉmytw*** between, among

***ỉmy r*** overseer

***ỉmw*** boat, ship

***ỉmw*** certain body parts

***ỉmn*** (god) Amun

***ỉmnyt*** daily offerings

***ỉmn, ỉmnt*** hide, secret, conceal

***ỉmnt*** secret place

***ỉmnt*** west, right side

***ỉmn*** right, right handed

***ỉmntỉ*** westerner (deceased)

*imntyw* westerners (deceased)

*imnty* western, right hand side

*imnty* west wind

*imntt* west, right side

*wnmy* right hand, right hand side

*imḥt* netherworld

*imsti* "**Imseti**" one of the sons of Horus

*imt pr* estate, property, will, testament

*imt nḏst* (boat's) stern

*imt ḥꜣt f* uraeus

*in*   *in* to, for, of, through, in, by (agent), because, not (etc) (see also ***n*** )

*in* by

*in* indeed

*in* says

*in* delay

*in* (a boat's) ropes

*ini* to bring, fetch, remove, carry off, bring about, overcome, reach, attain

*inyt* refrain (of song)

*inw* produce, quarry, gifts, tribute

*inw* matting

*inw* pattern, model

*inb* wall

*inb(t)* to wall off

*inp(w)* crown prince, royal child

*inpw* (god) Anubis

*ỉnm* skin

*n m, ỉn m* who, what

*ỉn m* wherewith?

*ỉnn* we

*ỉnr* stone, rock, block

- *ỉnr ḥḏ* limestone
- *ỉnr n mꜣṯ* granite
- *ỉnr n rwḏt* sandstone

*ỉnhmn* pomegranate

*ỉnḥ* surround, enclose

*ỉnḥ* eye brow(s)

*ỉn-ḥrt* (god) Onuris

*ỉnsy* red cloth

*ỉnḳ* envelop, embrace

*ỉnk* I, me, my

*ỉnt* bolti fish

*ỉnt* valley

*ỉnd, ỉnḏ* illness, ill

*ỉnḏ ḥr* hail to

*ỉr*

*ỉr* as for, as to, if

*ỉr* to, at, concerning, from, more than, so that, until, according as

*ỉrỉ* do, make, act, acquire, writing, achieving

- *ỉr-m* amounting to
- *ỉr(ỉ) m* act for (someone)
- *ỉr-n, ỉrt-n* engendered by, amounting to
- *ỉr(ỉ)-n* act on behalf of, help
- *ỉr(ỉ)-r* act against, oppose

*ỉri ḫt* rituals (lit. “doing things”)

*ỉryt* being done (or made), happened

*ỉry* relating to, belonging to

*ỉry ꜥꜣ* door keeper

*ỉry, ỉrw* from, thereof, thereto, make

*ỉryw* (boat's) crew

*ỉry nfr ḥꜣt* keeper of the diadem

*ỉry rdwy* attendant

*ỉry ḥmw* helmsman

*ỉry ḫt* administrator

*ỉry sšm* functionary

*ỉryt* dairy cow

*ỉryt* tax corn

*ỉrw* form, nature

*ỉrwy* eyes

*ỉr wdf* if (something) delays, ie, does not happen

*ỉrp* wine

*ỉrf* (gives emphasis to a command or question)

*ỉrr* doer

*ỉrt* duty, use, purpose

*ỉrt* eye

*ỉrwy* eyes

*ỉrt* (used for emphasis with "you")

*ỉrt* duty

*ỉrt* Yareth (in Syria)

*ỉrtyw* mourning

*ỉr ṯn* (used for emphasis with "you")

*ỉrtt, ỉrṯt* milk

*ỉh* *ỉhw* camp

*ỉhm* lag, go slowly

*ỉhm* hold back, detain

*ỉhhy* jubilation

*ỉḥ* *ỉḥ* ox, bull

*ỉḥ ḥmt* cow

*ỉḥ* net, snare, catch

*ỉḥ* palace

*ỉḥw* stable (for animals)

*ỉḥw* a measure of metal

*ỉḥwty* tenant farmer

*ỉḥms* occupant (in titles), attendant

*ỉḥms* sit down, dwell, besiege

*ỉḥmst* session of king and courtiers

*ỉḫ* *ỉḫ* then, therefore

*ỉḫỉ* to make flourish

*ỉḫm sk* indestructable

*ỉḫmt, ꜥḫmt* river bank

*ỉḫmt* ignorate ones

*ỉḫr* fall, defeated (see also *ḫr*)

*ỉḫḫw* dusk, twilight

*ỉḫt* thing(s)

*ỉs* *ỉs* indeed

*ỉs* go!

*ỉs* perish

*ỉs-ḥꜣḳ* plunder

*is* be old

*iswt* old times

*isywt* rags, old clothes

*is* chamber, tomb, workshop

*isi* be light (weight)

*isw* reeds

*isw* exchange, repay, reward

*(m) (r) isw* in return for

*is(w)t* gang, crew

*iswt* ancient times

*iswty* representative

*ispr* whip

*ispt* quiver (for arrows)

*ispt* throne

*isft* evil, wrongdoing, lie

*isfty* sinner

*isnii* are opened

*isr* tamarisk tree

*is-ḥȝḳ* plunder

*isḳ* linger,delay, restrain

*isk* Lo!

*ist* gang, crew

*ist* palace

*isṯ, ist* Lo!, Behold!, now

**iš** *išst* what?

*išt* property, belongings

*išd* **"ished"** tree (of life?)

*išd* fruit of the **"ished"** tree

*išdd* sweat

*iḳ* *iḳr* excellent, precious, virtue, trustworthy

*n iḳr* by virtue of

*r iḳr* exceedingly

*siḳr* advance, promote (a person), adorn (a place)

*(i)ḳd* build, fashion (pots)

*iḳdw* builders

*ik* *iky* stone cutter, miner

*i(ꜣ)kb* mourn

*ikm* shield

*ikn* draw (water)

*ig* *igrt* necropolis

*it* *it* father

*it nṯr* god's father (priestly class)

*it* barley, corn

*iṯi* carry off, seize, take possession of, remove, arrest, spend (time)

*iṯi ḥpt* proceed by boat

*iṯw* thief

*ity* sovereign

*ityt* queen regent

*itywn(y)* "welcome!"

*itm* (sun god) Atum

*itmw* lack of breath, suffocation

*itn* (god) Aten, sun's disk

***itn*** oppose, thwart

***itnw*** opponent

***itnw*** difficulties

, , (), ***itrw*** river, Nile

***itrw*** length of 6.5 mi

() () ***itrt*** row of sanctuaries

***itrt*** row of chapels

***itrt*** row of men

***itrt mḥt*** sanctuaries, or gods, of Lower Egypt

***itrt šmꜥ*** sanctuaries, or gods, of Upper Egypt

, ***itḥ*** drag, draw back (a bow), stretch, remove

***itḥ*** prison

*iṯ* ***iṯꜣ*** thief

, , ***iṯi*** carry off, seize, take possession of, remove, arrest, spend (time)

***iṯw*** thief

() ***iṯn*** (god) Aten, sun's disk

*id* ***idi*** be deaf

***idyt*** girl, maid

()(), ***idw*** pestilence

, , , ***idb*** bank, region

***idbwy*** the two banks, Egypt

() ***idmi*** red linenlace, serve instead of, proxy

***idn*** lay out

, ***idn*** replace, serve instead of, proxy

, ***idn*** serve as lieutenant commander

, , ***idnw*** deputy, substitute, overseer

, , , , ***idḥw*** Delta marshlands

***idḥy*** man from the Delta

***idr*** bandage, bind, stitch, stitching

[ ] ***idr[m]*** withhold [from]

, , ***idr*** herd of cattle

, , ***kꜣ n idr*** best bull (of the herd)

, ***idr*** herd of elephants

, ***idr*** flock [of geese]

***idryt*** punishment

( ) ***i(ꜣ)dt*** dew, pouring rain

, , , ***idt*** burnign incense, fragrance

, , ***idt*** fragrance

, , ***idt*** vulva, womb

, , ***idt*** cow

***y*** -  *-y* (suffix meaning having or being)

***ym*** 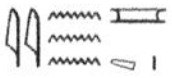 *ym* sea

***yn***  *ynʿm* Yenoam (in Palestine)

***yḥ***  *yḥ* Hey!

ꜥ

ꜥ arm, hand, region, condition, item

ꜥ cup

ꜥ warrant, certificate, record

ꜥ dyke

ꜥꜣ

ꜥꜣ here, there, yonder

ꜥꜣ ass, donkey

ꜥꜣ column

ꜥꜣ door

*ꜥꜣwy r* the two panels of a door

*iry ꜥꜣ* doorkeeper

ꜥꜣ great, many

*pr-ꜥꜣ* Pharaoh (lit - great house)

ꜥꜣ magnate, elder son

*ꜥꜣ(i)* be great, greatness

*ꜥꜣt* a great thing, greatness

*ꜥꜣw* greatly

*sꜥꜣy* make great, glorify

*ꜥꜣb* pleasant, pleasing, desirable

*ꜥꜣbt* self-seeking, selfishness

*ꜥꜣbt* food provisions

*ꜥꜣbt* offering, pile of offerings

*ꜥꜣm* throw stick

*ꜥꜣm* Asiatic

*ꜥꜣmw* Asiatics

*ꜥꜣmt* Asiatic woman

***ꜥꜣg*** flog, beat the feet of

, ***ꜥꜣt*** a valuable stone, stone vessel

***ꜥꜥ***

***ꜥꜥw*** to sleep

***ꜥꜥw*** ring

***ꜥꜥb*** cup

***ꜥꜥb*** to comb

***ꜥꜥny*** tent, camp

***ꜥw***

, , , ***ꜥw*** dragoman, translator

***ꜥwꜣ*** look after, care for

***ꜥwꜣi*** rob, steal, robber, one robbed

***ꜥwꜣy*** reap

***ꜥwꜥw*** ring

***ꜥwn*** defraud, rapacious, covetous, despoil

***ꜥwnt*** stick, club

, ***ꜥwt*** flock, herd, goats

***ꜥwt ḥḏt*** sheep (white flock)

***ꜥwt*** "**awet**" scepter

***ꜥb***

***ꜥb*** cup

, ***ꜥb*** unite

, , ***ꜥb*** horn, (archers) bow, cup

***ꜥb(ꜣ)*** shine, glitter

, ***ꜥbꜣ*** "**aba**" scepter

***ꜥbꜣ*** command

, , ***ꜥbꜣ*** stela, offering table

, ***ꜥbꜥ*** boast, exaggerate

***ꜥbꜥb*** to be excited

*ꜥbꜥb* threshold

*ꜥbꜥb* to appear, to shine

*ꜥbw* victims

, *ꜥbw* purfication, offerings

*ꜥbw r* breakfast

*ꜥbb* to knock (on a door)

*ꜥbt* fork

() ( ) *(i)ꜥbt ẖꜣt* burial

**ꜥp** *ꜥpr* Asiatics

, *ꜥpr* equip,learn, master, provide, acquire, incur, man

*ꜥprw* equipment

*ꜥprw* sailors

*ꜥprw* jewelry

*ꜥprw* workmen

**ꜥf** *ꜥfꜣy* encampment

*ꜥff* fly

*ꜥfnt* (royal) head-dress

, , , *ꜥfty* brewer

, *ꜥfdt, ꜥfḏt* chest, box

**ꜥm** , *ꜥm* to swallow, know

*ꜥm ib* to faint, lose consciousness

*ꜥm ib ḥr* be thoughtless, neglectful

*sꜥm* to swallow down, wash down (food)

*ꜥmꜥ* to smear

*ꜥmꜥ* mud

*ꜥmꜥꜣt* throw-stick

**ꜥn** , *ꜥn* beautiful, pleasing, kind

*ꜥn* a pleasant man

*iꜥn* baboon, sacred baboon

*ꜥnw* averted

*ꜥ(i)nw* the Turah limestone quarry

, *ꜥnn* turn back

*ꜥnḫ* sandal strap

*ꜥnḫ* garland

, *ꜥnḫ* live, life

*ꜥnḫ* mirror

*ꜥnḫ* person, citizen

, , *ꜥnḫ* captive

*ꜥnḫ* swear, oath

, , , *ꜥnḫw* the living

*ꜥnḫw* food

*ꜥnḫw* blocks (of alabaster)

*ꜥnḫt* (god's) eye

*ꜥnḫ-tꜣwy* Memphis

*ꜥnḫtt* means of subsistance

*ꜥnḫ ḏꜣ snb* life, prosrerity, health (for king)

, *wḥm ꜥnḫ* life (living) after death

*pr ꜥnkh* scriptorium

( )( ) *nb ꜥnḫ* sarcophagus

*sꜥnḫ* make to live, preserve, nurish

*sꜥnḫ* sculptor

, , , , *sḳr-ꜥnḫ* captive

*di ꜥnḫ* given life

*ꜥnḫwy* two ears

, *ꜥnḫt* goat

*ʿnḫt* corn

*ʿnḳt* (goddess) Anukis

*ʿnt* finger nail, claw

*ʿnty* god of 12th nome of Upper Egypt

*ʿntyw* myrrh

*ʿnd* few

**ʿr** *ʿr* reed (for writing)

*ʿr* pebble

*ʿr* ascend, mount, approach (see also *i͗ʿr*)

*sʿr* make to ascend, offer up

*ʿrw* neighborhood

*ʿrf* tie up, pack, envelop, bag

*ʿrr(w)(y)t* gate

*ʿrḳ* swear, take an oath

*ʿrḳ* understand

*ʿrḳ* know, perceive, wise, skilled, understanding

*ʿrḳ* put on (clothes), bent

*ʿrḳ [n]* bind [on]

*sʿrḳ* finish, complete, put an end to

*sʿrḳ* kill

*ʿrḳy* last day (of month)

*ʿrt* jaw

*ʿrt* hind quarters

*ʿrt* sheet or roll (papyrus or leather)

**ʿḥ** *ʿḥ* net, snare, catch

*ʿḥ* wipe off, wipe away

*ʿḥ* palace

*ꜥḥꜣ [r]* , fight [against]

*ꜥḥꜣ* warrior

*ꜥḥꜣ ḥnꜥ ... r* fight with ... against

*ꜥḥꜣ, ꜥḥꜣw* arrow

*ꜥḥꜣw* weapons, arsenal

*ꜥḥꜣwty* warrior

*ꜥḥꜣ-mw* sounding pole

*ꜥḥꜣt* battleground

*ꜥḥꜣt* warship

*ꜥḥꜣt* warriors

*ꜥḥꜣt, ꜥḥꜣ tw* beware lest

*sr-ꜥḥꜣ* challenge to battle

*ꜥḥꜥ* stand up, arise, stand fast, attend, come forth, erect, attend

*ꜥḥꜥ ib* persistent

*ꜥḥꜥn* at that time, in due time, waited, then (lit - stood by)

*ꜥḥꜥ ḥmsi* pass one's life

*sꜥḥꜥ* erect (an obelisk)

*ꜥḥꜥ* heap, proportion, allotment

*ꜥḥꜥ* quantity, wealth

*ꜥḥꜥ* beer measure

*ꜥḥꜥw* heaps

*ꜥḥꜥ ḥr* indulgent

*nb ꜥḥꜥw* wealthy man (lit - lord of heaps)

*rdi ꜥḥꜥ* produce

*ꜥḥꜥ* attendant

*ꜥḥꜥ* stela, station

*ʿḥʿ(w)* stela

*ʿḥʿw* stations, positions

*ʿḥʿw* period (of time), lifetime

*ʿḥʿw* service, attendance

*ʿḥʿw* helper

*ʿḥʿw* ships, the fleet

*ns-ʿḥʿw* overseer of ships

*ʿḥʿ ḥmsi* pass one's life (animals)

*ʿḥʿt* ships

*ʿḥt* field. holding, domain

*ʿḥwty* tenet farmer, field laborer

*ʿḥwtyw* tenet farmers, field laborers

**ʿḫ** *ʿḫ* brazier

*ʿḫi* hang up, raise up, hang

*ʿḫi* to fly

*ʿḫm* divine image

*ʿḫm* quench, extinguish, destroy

*ʿḫmt* river bank

*ʿḫḫw* dusk, twilight

*ʿḫt* swoop

**ʿẖ** *ʿẖi* to fly, fly away

*ʿẖm* divine image

*ʿẖm* voracious spirit

*ʿẖmw* branches

*ʿ ẖnwty* inner chambers, audience hall

**ʿš** *ʿš* call

*ꜥš* cedar, pine, fir

*ꜥšꜣ* lizard

*ꜥšꜣ* dove

*ꜥšꜣ* many, abundant, ordinary

*ꜥšꜣ ꜥšꜣ* very often

*ꜥšꜣt* multitude

*sꜥšꜣ* multiply

*ꜥšm* divine image

*ꜥš-ḥꜣt* pilot

**ꜥḳ**

*ꜥḳ [r][ḥr][m]* enter [into][before][among]

*ꜥḳ* trusted one (who can enter freely)

*ꜥḳ(yw)* intimates, friends

*ꜥḳyt* female servant

*sꜥḳ* cause to enter

*ꜥḳw* provisions, revenue (in food), loaves

*ꜥḳꜣ* be precise, accurate

*ꜥḳꜣ* adjust

*ꜥḳꜣ* equality, level

*ꜥḳꜣw* a rope

**ꜥg**

*ꜥgn* pedestal

*ꜥgt* varnish

**ꜥt**

*ꜥt* limb

*ꜥt* room, chamber, department

*iry ꜥt* department official

*ꜥtẖ* to strain (liquid)

**ꜥd**

*ꜥd* desert edge, limit of cultivation

*ꜥḏ, ꜥd* fat, grease

 ***ʿḏ*** spool, reel

 ***ʿḏ, ʿd*** be in good condition, be safe

 ***ʿḏ, ʿd*** perceive, recognize

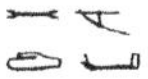 ***ʿḏ, ʿd*** hack up, excavate, cut out, destroy

***ʿḏ***  ***ʿḏ*** desert edge, limit of cultivation

 ***ʿḏ, ʿd*** fat, grease

 ***ʿḏꜣ*** guilty man, wrongdoer

 ***ʿḏꜣw*** guilty, guilt, crime

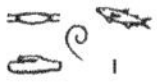 ***ʿḏw*** buri fish

 ***ʿḏ mr*** administrator (of a province)

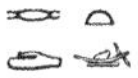 ***(m)ʿ(n)ḏt*** bark of the dawn

w  one, someone

      w  they, them, their

    𓇓, 𓇓𓈉  w  island

    𓅱𓈉, 𓅱𓊖  w  district, region

  - 𓅱𓏥  -w  (plural suffix)

    - 𓅱𓏏𓏥  -wt  (fem. plural suffix)

    - 𓅱𓏭  -wy  (dual suffix) two, pair of, very, twice

  - 𓅱  - w  (verb suffix) which, who, -ing

**wꜣ**  𓍯𓄿𓅱𓂻  wꜣ  far, distant, long

    𓍯𓄿𓅱𓂻 [𓂋]  wꜣi [r]  be far, afar, long ago, distant [from]

    𓏴, 𓏴𓂻, 𓊃𓍯𓄿𓅱𓂻, 𓊃𓍯𓄿𓏴, 𓊃𓍯𓄿𓅱𓂻, 𓊃𓍯𓄿𓂼  swꜣ  pass by, escape, surpass, pass away, remove, transgress, occur

    𓍯𓄿𓀁  wꜣi  to roast

    𓍯(𓄿)𓂻 (𓂼) [𓂋]  wꜣi [r]  fall [into]

    𓍯𓄿𓂝𓅱𓊛  wꜣʿw  captain (of ship)

    𓍯𓄿𓅱𓈗  wꜣw  wave

    𓍯𓄿𓅱𓏥  wꜣw  lassoes

    𓍯𓍯𓏏𓂝  wꜣwꜣt  coil of rope, cord

    𓍯𓍯(𓏭𓏭)𓈋  wꜣwꜣt  Northern Nubia, Kush

    𓍯𓄿𓍯𓄿𓏛  wꜣwꜣ  ponder, deliberate, take council

    𓄿𓂻𓈅  wꜣwt  Roads of Horus

    𓍯𓄿𓃀𓋳  wꜣb  cloth, swaddling clothes

    𓂻  wꜣr  fall into (a bad state)

    𓐎, 𓐎𓐎, (𓍯𓄿)𓐎𓐎(𓏤)(𓀉)  wꜣḥ  endure, place, permit, put down, discard, overlook, ignore, set up, sit for, be patient

    (𓍯𓄿)𓐎𓅓𓄣  wꜣḥ-ib  patient, well disposed

***swꜣḥ*** cause to endure

***wꜣḥyt*** sacred space

***wꜣḥyt*** corn

***wꜣḥw*** wreath, garland

***wꜣḥt*** processional station

***wꜣḫy*** palace reception hall, columned forecourt

***wꜣs*** dominion. lordship

***wꜣs*** "**was**" scepter

***wꜣsi*** be ruined, decay, ruin

***wꜣst*** (nome) Hermonthis, (city)Thebes (UE)

***wꜣsty*** the Theban

***wꜣš*** be exalted, be strong, be honored

***wꜣš*** extol

***wꜣg*** Wag festival

***wꜣg*** shouting

***wꜣt*** coil of rope

***wꜣt*** road, way, side

***r wꜣt*** path, passage

***swꜣ*** journey

***swꜣi*** pass by, escape, surpass, pass away, remove, transgress, occur

***tp-wꜣt*** journey, beginning (of reign)

***wꜣḏ*** papyrus

***wꜣḏ*** papyrus column

***wꜣḏ*** be green, fresh, vigorous

***wꜣḏ*** success, good fortune

***wꜣḏ*** fortunate man

*wꜣḏ* a green stone

*wꜣḏ wr* the sea (lit. - great green)

*wꜣḏt* green linen

*sw(ꜣ)ḏ* renew, hand over, bequeath

*wꜣḏyt* colonade

*wꜣḏyt* cobra godess (Wadjet)

*wꜣḏt* raw

*wꜣḏt* bow (of ship)

*w(ꜣ)ḏbw* shores

***wi*** *wi* I, me, my

*wi* I, me, my (god or king)

*wi* mummy, mummy wrap

*wiꜣ* sacred bark

*win* reject, decline

***wy*** *-wy* two, duality

***wꜥ*** *wꜥ* one, unique, alone

*wꜥi* be alone

*wꜥꜥw* privacy, solitude

*wꜥꜥwt* privacy

*wꜥꜥw* private appartment

*wꜥty* sole, unique, single

*wꜥꜣ* speak abuse, curse

*wꜥb* be pure, clean

*wꜥb* "**Wab**" (ordinary) priest

*wꜥbw* clean clothes, sacred robe

*wꜥbt* tomb, sanctuary, embalming place

***wꜥbt*** meat offering

***swꜥb*** purify, cleanse

, ***wꜥw*** soldier

() () ***wꜥf*** bend, curb

***wꜥn*** juniper

***wꜥr*** flee, fugitive

***wꜥrt*** flight

***wꜥrt*** leg, shank

, ***wꜥrt*** administrative district

() () ***wꜥrtw*** district offical

, ***wꜥḥ*** carob beans

***wꜥtt*** uraeus

***ww*** ***wwꜣb(wy)*** the Oxyrhychite nome

***wb*** ***wbꜣ*** open up, drill

, ***wbꜣ*** open courtyard

, ***wbꜣ*** butler

() () ***wbꜣ (ib) (ḥr)*** intelligent, capable, inlightened

[] ***swbꜣ ḥr [r]*** initiate [into]

***wbn*** overflow

***wbn*** walk quickly

, ***wbn*** shine forth, rise (sun)

***wbnw*** eastern

, , , ***wbnw*** wound, injury

***wbḫ*** be bright

() ***wbd(t)*** to burn, heat, scalded

***wp*** , , ***wpi*** divide, part, open, judge, discern, distinguish

***wpw ḥr*** except, but

***wp st*** specifically

***wpt*** specification

***wpt st*** specifically

***wp-wꜣwt*** (the wolf god) Wepwawet

***wpwt*** message

***wpwty*** messager, agent

***wpt*** brow, top (of head), beginning, vertex, horns

***wpt*** top knot

***wpt tꜣ*** earth's beginning, the extreme south

***wpt-rnpt*** New Years Day

***wpy*** decision

***wpš*** strew, scatter

***wpt-rnpt*** New Years Day

***wf*** ***wfꜣ*** talk, talk about, discuss

***wm*** ***wmt*** be thick

***wmt-ib*** stout hearted

***swmt*** make thick

***wmt*** gateway

***wmtt*** fortification, bullwork

***wn*** ***wn*** open, open up, rip open

***wn ḥr*** instructed, expert

***wn ḥr n*** enlightenment is given to

***wn*** fault, failing, blame

***swn*** perish

***wnỉ*** hasten, hurry, pass by, disregard

***wnw*** Hermopolis (Ashmunen) (UE)

***wnwn*** sway, travel about

***wnwt*** hour, priestly duties

***wnwt*** priesthood

***wnwt(y)*** hour watcher, astrologer

***wnpw*** triumph

***wnf*** be glad, happy

***wnm*** eat

***wnmt*** food, fodder

***wnmw*** food, sustenance

***wnm(w)t*** food

***wn-mꜣꜥ*** truth, reality

***wnmy*** right hand, right hand side

***wnmyt*** fire, devouring flame

***wnn*** exist, be

***wn-nfr*** Osiris

***wnt*, *wnnt*** indeed, really

***wn ḥr*** instructed, expert

***wn ḥr n*** enlightenment is given to

***wnḫ*** be clad

***wnš*** sledge

***wnš*** jackal or similar animal

***wnt*, *wnnt*** indeed, really

***wnt*** neglect

***wnḏw*** short horned cattle, goats

***wnḏwt*** subjects, people, associates

***wr*** ***wr*** great, much, many, very, greatness, sufficiency, excess, great one

***wr*** how much?

***wrr*** great, important, much

***wȝḏ wr*** the sea (great green)

***wr*** prince, great one, chief

***wr mȝw*** "greatest of seers" (priestly title)

***wr mḏ*** administrative title

***wrt*** great crown

***wrt*** greatness

***wrt*** the Great One (goddess)

***pr-wr*** national shrine of Upper Egypt

***mr-wr*** Menevis bull

***n-wr-n*** in as much as

***tȝ-wr*** larboard, west bank

***tȝ-wr*** the nome of Abydos

***wrỉ*** portion

***wryt*** door posts

***wrrt, wrryt, wryt*** chariot

***wrḥ*** ointment

***wrḥ*** anoint, be annointed with

***wrs*** head rest, pillow

***wrš*** spend all day, pass time

***wršy*** watchman, sentry

***ỉmy-wrt*** west side, starboard

***wrd , wrḏ*** to tire, be wear,y destroy

*wh* ***whȝt , wḥt*** cauldron

***whỉ*** escape, miss, fail

***wht*** failure

***whn*** overthrow

***swhn*** tear down

*wḥ* ***wḥꜣ*** pull up (a plant), hew (stone)

***wḥꜣt*, *wḥt*** cauldron

***wḥꜣt*, *wḥt*** oasis

***wḥyt*** village

***wḥyt*** tribe, tribesmen

***wḥꜥ*** loose, stop work , return

***wḥꜥ*** unravel, explain

***wḥꜥ*** fisherman. fowler

***wḥꜥ*** distribute rations

***wḥꜥ*** investigate

***wḥꜥ ib*** capable, skilled

***wḥm*** ass

***wḥm*** repeat

***m wḥm (ꜥ)*** a second time, again

***wḥm ꜥnḫ*** life (living) after death (lit - repeating life)

***wḥmw*** herald, reporter

***wḥmwty-f*** there will never be his like again

***wḥmt*** hoof

***wḥt*** cauldron

*wḫ* ***wḫ*** the nome of Cusae (UE), fetish of Cusae

***wḫ*** night, dark

***wḫt*** darkness, night

***wḫꜣ*** be or act ignorant or foolish

***wḫꜣ*** fool, incompetent

***wḫꜣ*** (wooden) column

***wḫꜣ*** hall of columns

***wḫꜣ*** require, demand

***wḫryt*** dockyard

***wḫd*** suffer, bear patiently, pain

***ws*** ***wsꞽr*** (god) Osiris

***wsf*** be idle, idleness, slack, sluggish

***wsr(w)*** oar

***wsrw*** oars

***wsr*** be powerful, wealthy, power, wealth

***wsr*** wealthy man

***ws(r)*** Thebes

***swsr*** make powerful

***wsrt*** neck

***wsḫ*** cup

***wsḫ*** collar

***wsḫ*** wide, broad, breadth, width

***wsḫt*** broad hall (of palace or temple), court

***swsḫ*** widen, extend, enlarge

***wsḫ(t)*** barge

***wsš*** die out

***wsš, wšš*** urinate

***wsšt*** urine

***wsṯn, wstn*** stride, move freely

***wš*** ***wš*** fall out, be bald, free, unoccupied

***gm wš*** found defective, destroyed

***wšꜣ*** fatten

***wšꜣ*** heap praises (on)

***wšʿ*** bite, chew

***wšb*** eat

***wšb*** answer

***wšb*** bull

***wšbw*** comforter

***wšm*** ear (of corn)

***wšmw*** beer jar

***wšn*** wring the neck of, make an offering of

***wšr*** dry up, be barren, be despoiled

***wšd*** address, question

***wg*** ***wgb*** rise

***wgg*** misery, want, weakness, feebleness

***wt*** ***wt*** to wrap, bandage

***wt*** bandage, embalm, mummy cloth

***wt*** embalmer

***wtȝw*** wrap, bandage

***wtḫ*** flee

***wtḫw*** fugitive

***wtt, wtṯ*** beget

***wṯ*** ***wṯtw*** offspring

***wṯs*** lift, carry, wear

***wṯsw*** those who have worn

***wṯst*** balance post

***wd*** ***wdỉ*** put, push, emit (a sound)

***wdỉ*** throw, shoot (an arrow), extend, place, put, commit, plant

***wdỉ*** to make (sound)

***wḏb, wdb*** turn, desist

***wdpw*** butler

***wdf, wḏf*** delay, lag, tardy

***wdn*** be heavy

***wdnt*** heavy stone

***wdn*** offer, make offerings, offering

***wdn*** offerer

***wdnw*** offerings

***wdrt*** region

***wdḥ*** pour out, pour off

**wḏ** ***wdḥ, wḏḥ*** cast (metal)

***wdḥw, wḏḥw*** table of offerings

***wḏ*** be a pilot

***wḏ*** jug

***wḏ*** inscription

***wḏ*** stela

***wḏꜣ*** be whole, sound, prosperous, uninjured

***wḏꜣw*** well-being, prosperity

***wḏꜣt*** eye of Horus

***swḏꜣ*** make healthy, keep safe

***wḏꜣ*** remainder

***wḏꜣ*** pectoral

***wḏꜣ*** magazine, storehouse

***wḏꜣ*** proceed, go, set out

***wḏꜣyt*** abode of Amen-Ra

***wḏꜣw*** amulets

***wḏi*** send forth, set forth

***wḏꜣ*** proceed, go, set out

***wḏyt*** (military) expedition

***wḏww*** wandering herds

***wḏ(t)*** to command, decree

***wḏ*** stela

***wḏ mdw*** to command

***wḏḏt*** what had been commanded

***swḏ* , *swd*** hand over, bequeath

***wḏꜥ*** divide, sever, judge between

***wḏꜥ-rwt*** judge

***wḏꜥt*** judgement

***wḏ-mdw*** to judge, litigate

***wḏꜥ*** open, discern

***wḏb*** turn, desist, turn back, fold over

***wḏb-ꜥ*** desist, gain composure

***wḏb*** sandbank, shore, river bank

***wḏf*** delay, lag, tardy

***wḏnw*** torrent, flood

***wḏḥ*** pour

***wḏḥ*** cast (metal)

***wḏḥ*** metal door

***wḏḥ*** wean, weaned child, weaned princeling

***wḏḥ*** weaned princeling

***wḏḥw*** table of offerings

**b** *b(w)* place, position

**bꜣ** *bꜣ* ram

*bꜣ* soul (in bird form)

*bꜣ* hack up, hoe (the earth)

*bꜣ* leopard skin

*bꜣw* boat

*bꜣw* spirits, might

*bꜣbꜣ* hole, hiding place

*bꜣbꜣt, bbt* flowing stream

*bꜣpfi* (god) Bapfi

*bꜣḥ* a measure of capacity

*bꜣḥ* foreskin, phallus

*m bꜣḥ ꜥ* in the presence of

*bꜣẖw* outlying region east or west of Egypt

*bꜣs* jar

*bꜣst* Bubastis

*bꜣstt* (cat godess) Bastet

*bꜣḳ* moringa tree

*bꜣḳ* moringa oil

*bꜣḳ* oily

*bꜣḳ* fortunate

*bꜣk* servant

*bꜣkw* work, task, decorated

*bꜣkbꜣk* a cake

*bꜣkt* work, task, labor, revenues, taxes

*bꜣgi* be remiss, slack, weary

***bȝgyw*** the dead

***b(ȝ)gsw*** dagger

***bȝt*** bush

***bi***

***biȝ*** copper, bronze

***biȝi*** of copper

***biȝy*** of bronze

***biȝ*** firmament, heaven

***biȝi, by [n] [ḥr]*** to wonder [at]

***biȝ(y)t*** wonder, marvel

***biȝyt*** wonders, marvels, miracle

***biȝw*** wonders, marvel

***biȝt*** marveling

***biȝty*** wondous person

***biȝw*** mine

***biȝw*** rare treasures

***biȝt*** quarry

***bin*** bad, miserable, act evilly

***bik*** falcon

***bik*** "Falcon" ship

***bit*** vase

***bit*** character, qualities

***bit*** bee

***bit*** honey

***bity*** king of Lower Egypt

***nsw bity*** King of Upper and Lower Egypt

***bꜥ*** — ***bꜥbꜥ*** drink

***bꜥbꜥt*** stream

***bꜥnt*** neck

***bꜥḥ*** abundance

***bꜥḥi*** be inundated, inundate, have in abundance

***bꜥḥ*** inundated land

***bw*** — ***bw*** hate, detest

***bwt*** abomination, detest

***bwytyw*** abominated ones

***bw*** place, position

***bwꜣw*** magnates

***bw bin*** misery

***bb*** — ***bbwt*** wig

***bbt*** flowing stream

***bn*** — ***bnw*** " **benu**" bird (pheonix), heron

***bnwt*** millstone

***bnbnt*** pyramidion

***bnn*** overflow

***bnn*** beget

***bnr*** dates

***ꜥt bnrt*** date-cake room

***bnrt*** date palm

***bnri*** sweet

***bnrt*** sweetness

***bnrw*** outside

***bnt*** harp

***bnty*** two baboons that greet the morning sun

**bh** — *bhꜣ* flee

*bhꜣw* fugitive

**bḥ** — *bḥ* forced labor

*bḥn* cut off (limbs), drive off (enemy)

*bḥs* to hunt

*bḥs* calf

*bḥdt* Behdet (LE), Edfu (UE)

*bḥdty* "winged sun disk" (lit - he of Behdet)

**bḫ** — *bḫn* tower, fortress

*bḫnt* pylon

**bs** — *bs* mystery, mysterious form, secret

*bs, ibs [ḥr]* introduce, enter [into], influx

*bsi* flow, come forth in abundance

*bsw* secret image

*bsw* flame

**bš** — *bšꜣ* malted barley

*bši* to vomit

*bšt, bšṯ* be rebellious, rebellion

*bšttyw* rebels

**bḳ** — *bḳ* be hostile

**bk** — *bkꜣ* be pregnant

*bkꜣ* tomorrow, morning

**bg** — *bgꜣw* shipwrecked man

*bgi* be remiss, slack

*bgs* bad, fractious

*bgsw* dagger

**bt** — *bṯ, bt* abandon, forsake, run

***btꜣ*** run

***btꜣ*** crime, wrong

***btꜣ*** wrong-doer

***btꜣt*** harm, injury

*bṯ* ***bṯn, btn*** be disobedient, defy

*bd* ***bd*** natron

***bdš*** faint, weak, exhausted, helpless, languish

***bdšt*** weakness

***bdt, bty*** emmer wheat

**p** — *p* base (for statue or shrine)

*p* Buto (LE)

**pꜣ** — *pꜣ* the, this

*pꜣ* fly

*pꜣy* he of

*pꜣy i* my

*pꜣ(w)* have done

*pꜣḳ* flat cake, biscuit

*pꜣḳt* fine linen

*pꜣwt* primeval times, antiquity

*pꜣwty* primeval god

*pss* results of labor

*pꜣt* bread offering, loaf

*pꜣd* knee

*pꜣḏ* a loaf

**pi** — *pis* tread in, bring in (corn)

**pꜥ** — *pꜥt* patricians, mankind

**pw** — *pw* that, this, whichever, who?, what?

*pwnt* Punt (Somalia)

*pwntyw* the people of Punt

**pf** — *pf, pfy, pfꜣ* that, yonder

*psi* to cook

*psw* preparation (of food)

**pn** — *pn* this, the

*p n* he of

*pnꜥ* upset, overturn

*pnꜥyt* cataract

*pnꜥnꜥ* roll over and over

*pnw* mouse

*pnḳ* bail out

*pr* *pr* house

*pryt* house (collective)

*pr-ꜥꜣ* Pharaoh (lit - great house)

, *pr-ꜥnkh* scriptorium

*pr-wr* national shrine of Upper Egypt

*pr-bity* palace

*pr-nbw* treasury (lit - house of gold)

*pr-nsw* palace

*pr-ḥḏ* treasury

*pr-ẖnty* harem

*pr-ḏt* estate

*ns pr n ḏꜣtt* steward of the estate

, , , *pri* battlefield

*ṯs-pri* fighting

*pri* go forth

*pr r ḫꜣ* go forth abroad

*pry* hero, champion

*pry* champion (ferocious) bull

*pr ꜥ* energetic, activity

, *prw* motion, procession, result

, *prw* excess, surplus

*prt* winter season

, *prt* procession

, , *prt* seed, fruit

***prt*** rising of Sothis

***prt-ḫrw*** voice (or votive) offering

***pḥ*** ***pḥ*** reach, attain, finish, attack, end by

***spḥ*** attain

***pḥwy*** hind quarters, back, rear-guard, end, stern

***pḥwy-r*** down to

***pḥwyt*** rectum

***pḥwyt*** stern-rope (of ship)

***pḥww*** marshlands, far north, distant marshlands, outer limits, ends of the earth

***pḥww m*** northward to

***pḥrr*** run

***pḥty*** strength, power

***pḥt r*** northward to, ending at

***pḥḏw*** chair

***pḫ*** ***pḫꜣ*** split, break open, purge, clean, reveal

***pḫꜣ*** pavement

***pꜣḫt*** a lion goddess

***pẖ*** ***pẖr*** turn, go round, serve

***pẖr wr*** Euphrates River

***pẖrt*** frontier guard

***pẖrt*** remedy, medicine, prescription

***pẖrty*** traveler

***pẖẖ*** control

***ps*** ***psi*** to cook

***psw*** preparation (of food)

*psn* a loaf

*psḥ* bite

*psḫ* be in disorder, distraught

*pss* results of labor

*psš* divide

*psš* division

*psšt* sharing out, share, portion, apportioning

*psg* spit, spit on

*psd, psḏ* shine

*psḏ* back, spine

*psḏntyw, psdn, psḏn* New moon festival

*psḏt* ennead, the nine gods

*pḏt, psḏt* The Nine Bows (a term for all of the traditional enemies of Egypt)

**pḳ** *pḳr* precinct of Osiris at AbyDos

*p(ꜣ)ḳt* fine linen

**pg** *pgꜣ* unfold, spread out, reveal

*pgꜣ* opening, mouth, entrance

*pgꜣ* bowl

**pt** *pt* sky, heaven

*pty* who? what?

*ptpt* trample down, crush

*ptr* who? what?

*ptr* behold!, see

*ptḥ* (god) Ptah

*ptḫ* overthrow, cast down, be stretched out

**pd** *pd* knee

*pd* kneel, run

, , , *pds* box

*pds* stamp flat

, , , *psḏ* back, spine

*pdswt* Delta dunes

***pḏ*** , , *pḏ, pd* stretch, be wide

*pḏw* spread out

*pḏt* (textile) measure

, *pḏt, psḏt* The Nine Bows (a term for all of the traditional enemies of Egypt)

, , , *pḏt, pdt* bow, foreigners, troops

*pḏt* foreign bowman, foreigner

*pḏt* troop

*ḥry pḏt* troop commander

*pḏty* bowman

# *f*

*f* he, him, his, it, its

*ỉp ḏt. f* grow up (id) (lit - count his self)

*n ḏt. f* his own

*ft* viper

**fꜣ**

*fꜣi* carry, lift, weigh

*fꜣi ṯꜣw* to sail (lit - carry the wind)

*fꜣw* magnificence

*fꜣw* food supplies

*fꜣk, fk* be bald, bare

**fn**

*fn* weak, infirm

*fnfnw* award compensation

*fnḫw* Syrian people

*fnḏ, fnd* nose

**fḫ**

*fḫ* loose, release, cast off, destroy, depart

**fḳ**

*fḳꜣ* cake

*fḳꜣ* reward

**fk**

*fk* be bald, bare (see also *fꜣk* )

**ft**

*ft* viper

*ft* disgust, show dislike

*ftft* leap

**fd**

*fdi* to pluck , remove

*fdḳ* tear asunder, piece, fraction

*fdt* sweat

**m** *m, ỉm* in, as, by, with, from, when, through, what

*m* behold

*m* who?, what?

*ỉn m* wherewith?

*r m* to what end?

*mỉ m* how?

*m [n k]* take [to yourself] (imperative)

*ỉmy* being

*ỉm* therein, there, thence

*ỉmy r* overseer

*m* (negative imperative)

*mꜣ* *mꜣ* end of a boat

*mꜣ-sḥꜣt* bow

*mꜣ-spḥw* stern

*mꜣꜣ* to see

*wr mꜣw* "greatest of seers" (priestly title)

*mꜣꜣw* sight

*mꜣw* aspect, appearance

*mꜣw* inspection

*mꜣỉ* lion

*mꜣw* lions

*mꜣ-ḥsꜣ* lion

*mꜣỉ(r), mꜣr* wretched

*mꜣỉ(r)w* misery

*mꜣꜥ* temple (of head)

***tp mꜣꜥ*** accompanying, escorting

***mꜣꜥ*** river bank

***mꜣꜥ*** real

***mꜣꜥ*** be true, real, loyal, righteous

***mꜣꜥ ḫrw*** true of voice, justified, deceased, triumphant

***smꜣꜥ ḫrw [r]*** triumph [over

***smꜣꜥ ḫrw [r]*** triumph [over]

***mꜣꜥ*** to offer

***mꜣꜥw*** offering, tribute

***mꜣꜥ*** send dispatch

***m mꜣꜥw nfr*** with a good wind, with good dispatch

***mꜣꜥt*** Maat

***ḥm-nṯr-mꜣꜥt*** prophet of Maat

***mꜣꜥt*** truth

***mꜣꜥtyw*** just man

***mꜣwy, mꜣ(w)*** be new, fresh

***mꜣwt*** new thing

***smꜣwy*** renew, renovate

***mꜣwt*** shaft

***mꜣwt*** rays (of light)

***mꜣr*** wretched

***mꜣḥ*** wreath

***mꜣḥḏ*** oryx

***mꜣḫ, mꜣẖ*** burn, be consumed

***smꜣ*** fighting bull

***mꜣst*** thigh, lap

***tp ḥr mꜣst*** in mourning (lit - head upon ones lap)

***mꜣgsw*** dagger

***mꜣt, mꜣṯ*** red granite

***inr n mꜣṯ*** granite

***mꜣṯ*** proclaim

***mꞽ*** — ***mꞽ*** Come!

***mꞽ, mr*** like, as well as, according to, as when, according as

***mꞽ*** (someone's) equal

***my, mꞽ*** likewise, accordingly

***mity, mitw*** like, equal

***mꞽ m*** how?

***miḫt*** the like

***mit(y)*** copy

***mity*** likeness

***mity, mitw*** like, equal

***mitt*** likeness, the like

***m-mitt*** likewise

***r-mitt-irw*** as well as

***smꞽ*** to report, announce, proclaim, acknowledgement

***mꞽ(w)*** waters

***miw, mit*** cat

***mibt*** axe

***mꞽ m*** how?

***min*** today

***minb*** axe

***m-ir*** do not

***m(i)niw*** herdsman

*miḥꜥt* tomb

*mist* liver

**my** *my, mi* likewise, accordingly

*myw* sperm

**mꜥ** *mꜥ* in the hand of

*mꜥ* together with, in the hand of, from, owing to

*m ꜥb* together with, in the company of

*mꜥ ntt* seeing that

*m ꜥbꜣ* harpoon

*mꜥnḏt* bark of the dawn

*mꜥr* be fortunate, successful

*mꜥḥꜥt, miḥꜥt* tomb

**mw** *mw* water

*mwy* urine, semen, saliva

*ḥr mw n* loyal to (lit - on the water of)

*mww* muu dancers

*mwnf* garrison

*mwt* weight

*mwt* mother, (goddess) Mut

*mwt* (goddess) Mut

*mwnf* helper, companion

*m(w)t* die

*mwt* mother

*mwt* (goddess) Mut

**mb** *m bꜣḥ (ꜥ)* in the presence of

**mf** *mfkꜣt* turquoise

**mm** — *m m* among, therein, there, thence, wherewith

*mmy* giraffe

**mn** — *mn* remain, be firm, be established, enduring, be fixed, stick fast, be attached, be vested

*m mn* at the rate of

*r mn* together with, as well as

*r mn m* as far as

*mn-nfr* Memphis (LE)

*smn* preserve, record,

*smn* establish

*smn* press down (bread)

*mn* be ill (of), suffer (from), miserable (about), troubled (about)

*mn* sick man

*mn, mnt* so and so, someone, such a one

*mni* death, die

*mni* pot

*mni* measure of capacity

*mni [m]* moor, land, attach, join

*mnit* mooring post

*mniw* herdsman, assault troops

*mniwt* harbour

*mnit* necklace (sacred to Hathor)

*mnꜥ* to nurse, suckle

*mnꜥy* male nurse, tutor

*mnꜥt* nurse, foster mother

*mnꜥt* milk cow

*mnit* necklace (sacred to Hathor)

***mnw*** kind of stone

***mnw*** monument, memorial

***mnwy*** abundant of monuments

, , , ***mnw*** trees, forest, plantation

***mnw*** mace

***mnw*** thread

, , ***mnw*** (god) Min

, ***mnnw, mnw*** fortress

***mnwt*** pigeon

, , ***mnfyt, mnfꜣt*** soldiers, assault troops

***mnfrt*** (arm) band

***mnmn*** move about, be disturbed

***mnmnt*** cattle, herds

, ***mnnw, mnw*** fortress

***mn nfr*** Memphis

***mnhd*** scribe's outfit

***mnḥ*** wax

***mnḥ*** papyrus plant

***mnḥw*** froth

***mnḫ*** be joyful

***mnḫ*** chisel, carve

, ()() ***mnḫ*** , be efficient, beneficent, potent, trusty, devoted, costly, excellent, splendid, thoroughly

***smnḫ*** advance, endow, confirm, restore

, ***mnḫ*** to string (beads), fasten

***mnḫw*** excellence, virtues

***mnḫt*** the third month

***mnḫt*** willingness

***mnḫt*** clothing, linen

***mnš*** cartouche

***mnḳb*** bed room (?) , cool place

***mnḳt*** jar

***m n k*** take [to yourself] (imperative)

***(m) mnt*** daily

***mnt*** such an amount, the like

***mnt*** so and so, someone, such a one

***mnt*** swallow (bird)

***mnt*** thigh, haunch

***mnṯw*** (god) Montu

***mnṯ(y)w*** Beduins of Asia

***mnḏ, mnd*** breast

***mnḏm*** basket, crate

***mr*** ***imy r*** overseer

***mr*** pyramid, tomb

***mr*** canal, channel, libation trough

***mrw*** harbors

***mr*** friends, partisans

***ḥꜣw mr*** the multitude, the masses

***mr*** bind

***mr*** ill, painful, sick, diseased

***mr*** a sick man

***mr ib n*** be sorry for

***mrw*** painfully

***mr ḥr ib n*** be displeasing to

***mrt*** pains, disease

***mrỉ*** love

***mrwt*** love, wish, will, desire

***m mrwt, n mrwt*** in order that

***mrw(y)ty*** the beloved

***mr-wr*** Menevis bull

***tꜣ mrỉ*** Egypt

***mryn*** Syrian warrior

***mryt*** river bank, coast, harbor

***mrw*** overseer of weavers

***mrw*** band

***mr(w)*** Syrian red "**meru**" wood

***mrw*** desert

***mr-wr*** sacred bull of Heliopolis

***m mrwt, n mrwt*** in order that

***mrw(y)ty*** the beloved

***mrrt*** street, avenue

***mrḥ*** decay

***mrḥt*** unguent, oil

***mrrt*** street, avenue

***mrkbt*** chariot

***mrt*** weavers, servants, underlings

***mrt*** serfs, slaves

*mh* [ ] ***[m] hꜣw*** [in] the neighborhood of, [at] the time of

***mhy*** be forgetful, negligent

***mhwt*** family, household

 ***mhr*** milk jug

***mḥ***  ***mḥ*** fill, inlay, pay in full, make whole,complete

 ***mḥ*** sieze, hold, capture

 ***mḥ-ib*** be trustworthy, trusted

 ***mḥ*** cubit (~20 inches), area(~ 275 sq ft)

 ***mḥ*** be anxious

 ***mḥ*** Lower Egytpian corn

 ***mḥi*** drown, launch (a boat)

 ***mḥ-ib*** be trustworthy, trusted

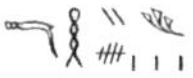 ***mḥy*** flax

 ***mḥyt*** fish

 ***mḥw*** fisherman

 ***mḥꜥ*** flax

 ***mḥw*** papyrus clump, lower Egypt, Lower Egyptian

 ***mḥyt*** north wind

 ***tꜣ mḥw*** Lower Egypt, the Delta, Lower Egyptian

 ***mḥ-s*** red crown of Lower Egypt

 ***mḥt*** Delta marshes

 ***mḥtt*** north

 ***mḥnyt*** uraeus, "the coiled one"

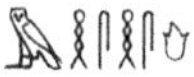 ***mḥsḥs*** filthy one

 ***mḥt*** bowl, dish

 ***mḥt*** fan

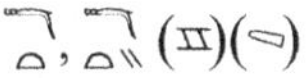 ***mḥty*** northern, northward, north

 ***mḥtyw*** northerners

***mḫ***  ***mḫꜣ*** to balance, equal *mḫꜣt* balance, scale

*m ḫmt* in the absence of, without

*smḫ* forget

*m ḫt* after, afterward, accompanying

*mḫtbt* an ornament

*m-ḫdi͗* northward

**mḫ** *mḫꜣ* incline (to do)

*mḫnt* ferry boat

*mḫnty* ferry boat operator

*mḫr* storehouse

*mḫr* low-lands

*mḫrw* administration, governance, business

**ms** *ms* bouquet

*ms* No! (expresses surprise or reproof)

*i͗w ms* Indeed not!, misstatement

*ms* bring, present, bring away booty, extend (aid), take aim

*msi͗* give birth, form, fashion

*ms* born of

*ms n, mst n* born to

*ms* child

*msꜣ* young recruits

*mswt* birth

*mswt* young children or animals

*mswtt* girl child

*mstiwty* descendant of a god

*smsi͗* deliver (a baby)

***msy*** last

***msyt*** make a festival

***msyt*** supper, evening meal

***msbb*** to turn

***msn*** Mesen (LE)

***msnw*** harpooner, hippopotimus hunter

***msnḥ*** turn backward

***msḥ*** crocodile

***msḫn*** abode of the gods

***msḫtyw*** adze

***msḫtyw*** Great Bear constellation

***mss*** totter

***mss*** tunic

***mss*** corselet

***msštꜣ*** frame (of chariot)

***msḳ*** leather

***msḳt*** the Milky Way

***mskꜣ*** hide, skin

***mskỉ*** rumor

***msktw*** armlet

***msktt*** bark of the evening

***mst*** staff

***mst*** fox skin apron

***mstỉwty*** descendant of a god

***mstw*** offspring

***mstpt*** funeral bier

***msdmt, msḏmt*** kohl, black eye paint

***msḏḏt*** what is hateful

***msḏi, msdi*** to hate

***msḏr*** ear

***msḏrwy*** the two ears

**mš** ***mšꜥ*** army

***mšꜥ*** expedition

***mšw*** sword

***mšrw*** evening

***mšdt*** ford

**mk** ***mki*** to protect, guard, look after

***mkt*** protection

***mk*** behold!

***mkḥꜣ*** to neglect

***mkt*** right place

**mg** ***mgꜣ*** skirmisher

***mgꜣ*** yougn recruits

**mt** ***mt, mṯ*** behold!

***mt*** vein, muscle, vessel of body

***mt*** strip (of cloth)

***mt*** die, death

***mty*** precise, straightforward, correct, loyal, trustworthy, regular, customary, exactness

***mtyt*** rectitude

***mtwn, mṯwn*** combat venue for bulls

***mtwt*** semen, poison

***mtpnt*** dagger

***mtmt*** discuss

***mtn, mṯn*** behold!

***mtn*** reward

***mtnwt*** reward

***mṯn, mtn*** road

***mtn, mṯn*** nomad hunter

***mtr*** fame, renown

***mtr*** bear witness to, testify concerning

***mtrw*** witness

***mtrw*** witnesses

***mtrt*** midday

***mtt n ib*** rectitude, affection

***m mtt nt ib-f*** following his heart

***mt, mṯ*** behold!

***mṯ***

***mṯꜣ*** to flout, insult

***mṯꜣm*** sheer dress

***mṯꜣt*** land inheritance

***mtwn, mṯwn*** combat venue for bulls

***mṯn*** Mitanni (East of the Euphrates)

***mṯn, mtn*** road

***mtn, mṯn*** nomad hunter

***mtn, mṯn*** behold!

***md***

***mdw*** walking stick, staff, supporter

***mdw*** speak, recite, word, talk, speech, plea

***wḏ mdw*** give command

***mdw ḥr*** speak to, litigate about

***mdw m*** speak against

***mdw ḥnꜥ*** dispute with, litigate against

***mdwty*** speaker

***mdt*** speech, words

***mdw nṯr*** the god's words

***ḏd mdw in*** speech by, words spoken by

***ḏd mdw*** recitation, speech (continued)

***mdḥ*** hew

***mds*** keen, alert, sharp

***mdt*** word

***mḏ*** ***mḏ*** be deep

***mḏꜣw*** Medja in Nubia

***mḏꜣyw*** Medjay from Medja

***mḏꜣbt*** one who bails out a boat

***mḏꜣt*** papyrus scroll, book

***mḏꜣt*** sculptor's chisel

***mḏw*** ten

***mḏwt*** stables

***mḏt*** stabled cattle

***mḏr*** shut out

***mḏḥ*** fillet (headband)

***mḏḥ*** hew

***mḏḥw*** carpenter, shipwright

***mḏḥt*** headband

***mḏt*** deep, depth

***mḏt*** oil, ointment

***mḏt*** stable, cattle stall

***mḏd*** hit (a mark), stay on (a path), press on

# n

*n* we, us, our

*n, in* to, for, of, through, in, because, not (etc)

*n, nn* not, cannot, if not, unless, no, without, none, (negates)

*-n* (past tense - suffix)

## nꜣ

*nꜣ* this, these, the

*nꜣw* breeze

## ni

*niꜣw* ibex

*ni* reject, drive away, rebuff, get rid of, throw down

*niw, nww, nw, nnw, nwnw* primeval waters

*niw* bowl

*niw* ostrich

*niwiw* be glad

*niwt* village, town, Thebes (lit - the City)

*niwty* local

*niwty* local folk, townsmen

*n(iw)tyw* those in the lower heaven

*nis* invoke, summon, recite

*nisw* one summoned

*nik* serpent demon

*nit* wrong doing

## ny

*ny, nw, n* therefore, for

*ny* them, they, we two, us two, our

*nyny* to do homage, greeting

*ny sw* he belongs to

## nꜥ

*nꜥi* to sail, to travel by boat

*nꜥyt* mooring post

***nꜥw*** serpent

***nꜥꜥ*** smooth

***nꜥt*** expedition

**nw**

***nw*** be weak, limp

***nw*** weakness

***nw*** see, look

***nw*** hunter

***nw*** this, these

***nw*** time

***nw, nyw*** of

***nw*** produce, quarry, gifts, tribute

***nwꜣ*** see, look

***nwỉ [r]*** return [to]

***nwy*** return, come, bring back

***nw(i)*** collect, tend, assemble

***nwy*** return, come, bring back

***nwy*** water, flood

***nwyt*** waters of a river, canal, etc

***nww, nwnw*** primeval waters

***nwḥ*** rope

***nwḥ*** to bind (enemies)

***ink, nwk*** I, me, my

***nwt*** (sky goddess) Nut

***nwt*** adze

***nwtỉ*** the two adzes

***nwd*** turn aside, vacillate, move crookedly, aslant

***nwd*** ointment, perfume

*nwdw* act improperly

*nwdw* unguents

*nwdwt* squeeze out

**nb** *nb* every, all (used after modified word)

*rʿ nb* every day

*nb* lord, master, owner (of) (used before modified word)

*nb ʿnḫ* sarcophagus

*nbt* lady

*nbt* lordship, authority

*nbȝ* pole

*nbỉ* to swim

*nbỉw* unit of linear measure > 1 cubit

*nbyt* beaded collar

*nbyt* Kom Ombo (UE)

*nbw* gold

*nbỉ* to gild,fashion

*nby* gold smith

*nbwy* the Two Lords (Seth and Horus)

*nbwt* aegean islands

*nbnb* guard

*nbs* a thorn tree

*nbt* Ombos (UE)

*nbt* basket

*nbty* The Two Ladies (king's title)

*nbt-ḥt* (goddess) Nephtys

*nbdw ḳd* perverse (enemy)

*nbḏ* destructive

**np** *npri* (corn god) Nepri

*nprt* edge, brim

**nf** *nf* wrong

*nf, nfꜣ* that

*nfꜥ* remove, drive away

*nfw* skipper, captain (of boat)

*nfr* good, perfect, beautiful, happy, happily, well

*mn-nfr* Memphis (LE)

*nfr* goodness, perfection, beauty, good fortune

*nfrw* goodness, perfection, beauty, end

*nfr* zero

*nfrw* shortage, deficiency

*nfryt* end, bottom, until

*nfryt* tiller rope

*nfryt r* down to

*nfrw* innermost room

*nfrw* recruits

*nfr* crown of Upper Egypt

*nfr-ḥḏt* crown of Upper Egypt

*nfr n i* I died (lit - happy for me)

*nfrt* good things, what is good, kindness

*nfrt* cattle

*nfrt* fair woman

*nft, ntf* loose, slacken

*nft* to breathe

*snf* make to breathe, succor, unload (a boat), empty out (contents), relieve, release

₃ i y ʿ w b p f m **n** r h ḥ ḫ ẖ s š ḳ k g t ṯ d ḏ

𓃀𓄿𓂻 ***nftft*** leap

**nm** ***n m, in m*** who?, what?

***nm*** go wrong, stea

***nm*** knife

***nmt*** slaughter house

***nmi*** traverse, travel

***nmi*** cry aloud, lowing (of cattle)

***nmʿ [n]*** show partiality [to], question

***nmw*** vats

***nmḥ*** be poor, deprive (of)

***nmḥ(y)*** orphan, low class person

***nms*** "**Nemes**" royal head-dress

***nmst*** water jug

***nmtt*** step, walk,, stride, actions, procedures

***nmtt*** walk, steps

***nn*** not, cannot, if not, unless, no, without, none, (negates)

***nn*** this, these

***nni*** be weary, tired, slothful

***nni-nsw*** Heracleopolis (UE)

***nwnw, nnw*** primeval waters

***nnm*** go wrong

***nnšm*** spleen

***nnk*** mine, on my part

***nnt*** rushes

*nr*

***nrꜣw*** ibex

***nr*** charge (an enemy)

***nr i*** to protect

***snr*** take care of

***nri*** be in terror

, , ***nrw*** terror

***nrw*** terrible one

***snr*** terrify

, ***nrt*** vulture

*nh*

***nhy*** little, few, some

, ***nhw*** loss, escape

***nhw*** protection

***nhwt*** trees

()() ***nhp*** to care (for)

***nhp*** rise early

***nhpw*** early morning

***nhm*** jubilate, shout, thunder

, ***nhrn, nhꜣrynꜣ*** Naharin (Eastern Mesopotamia, between the Tigris and Euphrates rivers)

***nhs*** to wake up

***nht*** sycamore-fig

***nht*** shelter

*nḥ*

***nḥ*** guinea fowl

***nḥꜣ*** shake

***nḥꜣ*** be hard, rough, dangerous, contrary, perverse

, , () ***nḥi*** pray (for)

***nḥt*** prayer

***nḥb*** yoke together, unite

*nḥbw* yoked oxen

*nḥb-kȝw* (a serpant diety)

*nḥbt* neck, shoulder

*nḥbt* lotus bud

*nḥp* potter's wheel

*nḥm* take away, rescue

*nḥmn* surely, assuredly

*nḥn* rejoice

*nḥr* resemble

*nḥḥ* eternity, forever

*nt nḥḥ* of eternity, for eternity

*nḥsy* Nubian

*tȝ-nḥs(y)* Nubia

*nḥdt* tooth

*ndḥt, nḥḏt* tusk

*nḫ* — *nḫ* to defend, protect, protection

*nḫwt* complaint, mourning

*nḫb* stipulation

*nḫb* open (for use)

*nḫb* fresh land

*nḫbt* germination, shooting up

*nḫbt* titulary, protocol

*nḫb* **"Nekheb"** (El Kab) (UE)

*nḫbt* (godess) Nekhbet

*nḫn* be young, child

*snḫn* to nurse

*nḫnw* youth

*nḫn* **"Nekhen"** (Hieracompolis) (UE)

*nḫḫw* flail

*nḫt* strong, victory, victorious, strength, mighty

*nḫtw* stength, victories

*nḫtt* victory

*snḫt* to strengthen

***nḫ*** *nḫnm, nšnm* oil vase

***ns*** *ns* tongue

*st-ns* speech

*ns* flame

*nswt* flame, fire

*nsr* burn, blaze

*nsrt* flame

*nsy* be king

*nsyw* kings

*nsyt* kingship

*ns-ꜥḥꜥw* overseer of ships

*ns pr n ḏꜣtt* steward of the estate

*nsw* he belongs to

*nsw, ni-swt* king of Upper Egypt, king

*nsw ẖkryt* king's ornament (concubine title)

*n-sw-bit* King of Upper and Lower Egypt

*nsrt* (uraeus goddess) Nesret, uraeus, royal serpent

*nsb* lick

*nss* do damage

*ns-sḏꜣwty* chief treasurer

***nst*** seat, throne

***ḫrp nsty*** controller of the two seats

***nst*** cut(?)

***nsty*** a type of bread

**nš** ***nš*** supplant, drive away, expel

***nšy*** dress (hair)

***nšt*** hair-dresser

***nšp*** breathe

***nšmt*** fish scale

***nšmt*** bark of Osiris at Abydos

***nšny, nšni*** rage, storm, foul weather, disaster

***nš ḥr*** supplant, drive away [from]

**nḳ** ***nḳꜥwt*** notched sycamore figs

***nḳm*** be in pain, sorrow, suffer

***nḳdd*** sleep

**nk** ***nk*** copulate

***nkꜣ [m]*** reflect [upon], think [about]

***nkꜣt*** plot

***nkn*** sword

***nkn*** damage, injure

***nkt*** matter, trifle, little

**ng** ***ng*** bull

***ngi*** break open

***ngt*** breach

***ngmgm*** conspire

***ngsgs*** overflow

***ngt*** breach

***nt*** *nt* half month festival

*nt* red crown of Lower Egypt

*nt* water

*ntf* to water, irrigate, sprinkle

*nt, nrt, nit* (goddess) **Neith**

*nty* who, which

*ntf, nty f* which he

*n(iw)tyw* those in the lower heaven

*ntꜥ* custom, observances

*ntb* be parched

*nt pw* it is the fact that

*ntf* he, his

*ntf* loose, slacken

*ntf* which he

*ntf* to water, irrigate

*nt nḥḥ* of eternity, for eternity

*nts* she

*ntsn* they

*ntk* you, yours

*ntk, ntyk* which you

*ntt* that

*mꜥ ntt* seeing that

*r-ntt* in-as-much-as, in that

*ḥr ntt* because

*ntṯ, ntt* you

*ntṯn, nttn* you

***nṯ*** *nṯr* god, divine

*it nṯr* god's father (priestly class)

*nṯry, nṯr(i)* be divine

*nṯrt, ntrt* goddess

*nṯr nfr* the perfect god (king's title)

*ḥm nṯr* prophet, high priest

*ḥtp(w)-nṯr* divine offerings

*ẖrt nṯr* necropolis

*ẖrtyw-nṯr* necropolis workmen

*snṯr, sntr* incense

*šwyt* god's image

*tꜣ nṯr* vassal state (lit - god's land)

***nd*** *ndb* sip

*ndb [m]* cover [with]

*ndbw* band (a door)

*ndbwt* area, full extent

***nḏ*** *nḏ* ask, inquire

*nḏwt r* counsel, consultation

*nḏnḏ* take counsel

*nḏ r* take counsel, consult, question

*nḏ ḥr* confer [on], greet

*nḏ ḫrt* greet, pay one's respects

*nḏt ḥr* gifts, homage

*nḏ* thread

*nḏ [m ꜥ]* save [from]

*nḏ* grind, miller

*nḏ* protect

 ***nḏty*** protector

 ***nḏꜣ*** be parched, stifled

 ***nḏꜣ*** be parched, stifled

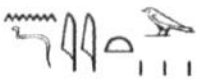 ***nḏyt*** baseless

 ***nḏw*** miller

 ***nḏwt-r*** counsel, consultation

 ***nḏm*** "**nedjem**" or carob tree

 ***nḏm*** sweet, agreeable, pleasant, well, comfortable

 ***nḏm ỉb*** joyful

 ***nḏ [m ꜥ]*** save [from]

 ***nḏrỉ*** to hold fast, catch, arrest, obey, follow, draw tight, take possession of

 ***nḏrt*** imprisonment

 ***nḏḥt*** tusk

 ***nḏs*** small, poor, feeble, dim

 ***nḏs*** poor man, commoner, citizen, man

 ***nḏsw*** poverty, low estate

 ***nḏt*** subjects, serfs

 ***ndty*** protector

 ***ndtyw*** maid-servants

**r** *r, ỉr* to, at, concerning, from, more than, so that, until, according as

*r* part, 1/320 "**hekat**" measure

*r* mouth , spell, door, opening, speech, language

*r* a type of goose

**rꜣ** *rꜣw* Turah (limestone quarry site)

*rꜣw-f* entire, all

**rỉ** *r ỉ* (gives emphasis to "I")

*r-ỉwd ... r* between ... and

*rỉt* side

**rꜥ** *r ꜥ* place, state

*rꜥ* (god) Ra, sun

*rꜥ* (god) Ra

*rꜥ nb* every day

*rꜥt* sun goddess (said of queen)

*sꜣ rꜥ* son of Ra (the king)

*rꜥ-ḥr-ꜣḫty* (god) Ra Horakhty

*r-ꜥ* end, limit, near, likewise

*r ꜥ ꜥ* beside, near

*rꜥwy* hands (or their activities)

*r-ꜥ-ḫt* combat, war

*ḫꜥw-nw--r-ꜥ-ḫt* weapons of war

*r-ꜥḳꜣ* on a level with

**rw** *rw* lion

*rwty* lion's den

*rwty* the Two-lion god

***r wꜣt*** path, passage

***rwꞽ*** wander

***rwꞽ*** dance

***rwꞽ [r]*** cease, make to cease, depart [from]

***rwy*** 2/3

***rwt*** gate, door

***rwty*** double gate or door

***rwty*** outside

***rwyt*** judgment hall

***rwdw*** stairway

***r(w)d*** be strong

***rwd*** strength, firmness

***rwḏ*** hard, firm, strong, enduring, succeed

***rwḏ*** string, bow string

***rwḏ*** control, administer, controller, executor

***rwdw*** agent

***rwdt*** success

***rwdt, rwḏt*** hard stone, sandstone

***ꞽnr n rwḏt*** sandstone

***rp*** ***r pʿt*** hereditary prince

***rpyt*** statue of female

***r pw*** or

***r-pr*** temple, chapel

***(r) pḏt*** foreign bowmen

***rf*** ***rf*** (gives emphasis to a command or question)

***rm*** ***r m*** to what end?

***rm*** fish

***rmw*** fish, fishy smell

***rmi*** to weep, beweep

***rmwt*** tears

***rmw*** weeping

***r-mitt-irw*** as well as

***rmn*** arm, shoulder, side, to carry

***rmn*** total

***r mn*** together with, as well as

***r mn m*** as far as

***rmn*** (measure of) 1/2 aroura

***rmn*** processional shrine

***rmnn*** Lebanon

***rmrm*** chastise

***rmṯ,*** man, men, mankind, people

***rn***

***rn*** name

***rn*** name (of king)

***rn*** young (animal)

***rny*** calf

***rnp*** colt

***rnp*** young man

***rnpi*** be young, vigorous

***rnpw*** youthful vigor

***rnpwt*** vegetables, herbs

***rnpt*** year

***wpt-rnpt*** New Years Day

***ḥȝt-sp*** regnal year

*tp-rnpt* feast of the first of the year

*rnn* rejoice, exalt

*rnn* caress

*rnn* nurse, raise (a child)

*rnnt* wet nurse

*rnnt* nurse goddess

*rnnwtt* harvest goddess, name of 9th month

*r-ntt* in-as-much-as

***rr*** *rri* pig

*rrt* sow

***rh*** *rhn [ḥr]* lean [on], rely, tread [on], drive [in]

*rhdt* jar, vat, cauldron

***rḥ*** *r-ḥꜣt* mouth (of river)

*rḥw* men, fellow

*rḥwy* two combatants

*rḥwy* Ra & Thoth or Horus & Seth

*r-ḥry* master chief

***rḫ*** *rḫ* to know , learn

*rḫ* wise man

*srḫ* complain, accuse

*srḫ* learn about

*rḫyt* common people

*dwꜣ rḫyt nb* all the common people give praise

*rḫḫy* celebrated

*rḫs* to slaughter

*rḫt* amount, number, knowledge

***rḫt*** to wash (clothes)

***rḫty*** washerman

***rḫtt*** the ends of the earth

*rs* ***rs*** (used for emphasis) indeed!

***rs*** be wakeful, be vigilant

***rsw*** sentry, vigilance

***rs tp*** vigilant

***srs*** awaken, assume command

***di-rs-tp*** foremam

***rsy*** south, southern

***rsw*** south wind

***rswt*** south land

***rswt*** south

***rs(y)w*** southerners

***rsf*** catch (of prey), affluence

***r ssy*** entirely, quite, at all

***rst*** sacrificial victims, foreign hordes

*rš* ***r-sṯꜣw*** necropolis (of god Sokar)

***rš(w)*** rejoice

***ršwt*** joy

***ršršt*** rejoice

*rḳ* ***rḳ*** to incline, bend, defy

***rḳ ib*** disaffected one, rebel

***rḳw*** tilting, enmity

***rḳw*** enemy

***rḳt ib*** ill will, envy, hostility

**rk**

*rk* (used for emphasis with "you")

*rk* time, period

*rkḥ* burning, heat, light

*rkḥ* the burning festival

*rkḥt* heat

**rt**

*rtḥ* restrain

*rtḥty* baker

*rṯn, rtn* whither

*r tnw sp* every time that

*rtt* conspiracy

**rṯ**

*rṯ* (used for emphasis with "you")

*rmṯ, rmṯt* man, men, mankind, people

*rmṯt* mankind, people

*rṯn* (used for emphasis with "you")

*rṯn, rtn* whither

*rṯnw* Retjnu (Syria)

*rmṯ* man, men, mankind, people

**rd**

*rd* foot

*rdwy* the two feet

*st-rd* rank

*tp-rd* instructions, rules, principless

*rd* make to grow, flourish

*srd* to grow, to erect

*rdw* stairway

*r(w)d* be strong

*r-ḏr-f* entire

*di, rdi* to give, place, cause, grant

***rd(i)*** who causes

***rdỉ ỉb m-sꜣ*** be anxious about

***rdỉ ỉb ḫnt*** pay attention to

***rdỉ ꜥḥꜥ*** produce

***rdỉ m ỉb*** determine

***rdỉ m ḥr*** command

***rdỉ r tꜣ*** to land, throw down, neglect

***rdỉ ḥr gs*** partial, bias, dispose of, kill

***rdỉt n r ḥr s*** "without neglecting my orders"

***rdnỉw*** share, portion

**rḏ** ***rḏꜣw*** fight, battle

, , ***r ḏꜣwt*** in return for, because of

, ***rḏw*** efflux

, ***r ḏd*** saying that

# *h*

*h* **room**

***hꜣ***

*hꜣ* Ha, Ho

*hꜣꞽ* come down, go down, descend, grasp (meaning), fall, charge down, drip, drop, tackle, befall, attack

*shꜣꞽ* send down, cause to fall

*hꜣy* husband

*hꜣyt* portal (see also *hyt*)

*hꜣw* environment, neighborhood, time

*hꜣw* neighbors, kindred

*m hꜣw* in the neighborhood of, at the time of

*hꜣb* penetrate

*hꜣb [n] [ḥr]* send [to] [about]

*hꜣbt* dance

*hꜣrt* herds (of animals)

*hꜣkr* "**Haker**" feast

*hꜣt* ceiling

***hꞽ***

*hꞽ* husband

*(m) hꞽ ms* approaching in a humble manner

***hy***

*hy* Hail!, shout

*hy hnw* jubilate

*hꞽ, hy* husband

*hyt* portal

*smsw hyt* elder of the portal

***hb***

*hb* enter, penetrate into, travel

*hbhb* traverse, explore, travel

***hb*** ibis

***hb*** plough

***hbi*** tread out, travel

***hbny*** ebony

***hbnt*** "**hebnet**" (liquid) measure, a jar

***hbny*** ebony

***hp*** ***hp*** law

***hm*** ***hmt*** fare, payment to ferryman

***hmhmt*** roaring, war cry, squaking

***hn*** ***hn*** box, chest

***hn*** halt

***hnw*** "**henu**" measure ( ~1/2 quart)

***hnw*** jubilation, praise

***hy hnw*** jubilate

***hnw*** neighbors, associates, family

***hnn*** deer

***hnn*** nod, bow, attend to

***hnn [n][ḥr][m]*** rely [on]

***hr*** ***hr(i)*** be content, pleased, quiet

***hrt*** contentment

***hr ti*** you are content

***shri*** make content, bring peace

***hrw*** day, day time

***hrwyt*** day book, journal

***ẖrt-hrw*** daytime, daily

***hrp*** sink, be submerged

***hrp ib*** suppress thoughts

*hrmw* enclosure for birds, pen

***hh*** *hh* hot breath, blast of heat

***hs*** *hsmḳ* wade

***hḳ*** *hḳs* be deficient, stint, steal

***ht*** *ht* portal

***hd*** *hd* punish, defeat, attack

*hdmw* footstool

*hdhd* (army) charge

**ḥ** — *ḥwi* surge up, overflow, rain

*ḥwi, ḥii* strike, beat, drive in, tread (a road), hit

**ḥꜣ** — (…)(…) *ḥꜣ* (desert god) Ha

*ḥꜣ* would that!

*ḥꜣ* back of head, behind, around

*ḥꜣ* outside

*pr r ḥꜣ* go forth abroad

*ḥꜣi* mourn

*ḥꜣy* naked

*ḥꜣwy* naked man

*ḥꜣwt* nakedness

*sḥꜣy* lay bare, expose, reveal

*ḥꜣyw* carrion-birds

*ḥꜣw* excess

*rdi ḥꜣw ḥr* increase

*m ḥꜣw* in excess of

*m ḥꜣw ḥr* in addition to, except

*ḥꜣw mr* the multitude, the masses

*ḥꜣꜥyt* strife, discontent, civil war

*ḥꜣꜥb* bad quality

*ḥꜣw-mr* the lower orders

*ḥꜣw-ḫt* special offering

*ḥꜣwty* the foremost

*ḥꜣp* conceal, hide, secret mysterious

*ḥꜣp* secret place

*ḥꜣm* catch fish or fowl

*ḥꜣḳw* captives

*ḥꜣḳ(t)* plunder, capture, carry off

*ḥꜣt* tomb

*ḥꜣt* front, fore, foremost, vanguard, van , forward

*[m] [r] [ẖr] ḥꜣt* in front of, before

*ẖr ḥꜣt* in front of, before, formerly

*imy ḥꜣt* prototype, example, pattern, who is in front, which is in front

*imyw-ḥꜣt* ancestors

*ḥꜣt ꜥ [m]* beginning [of]

*ḥꜣty* heart, breast

*ḥꜣty-ꜥ* the finest of

*ḥꜣty ꜥ* local prince, nomarch, mayor

*ḥꜣtwy-ꜥ* local princes, mayors

*ḥꜣt-sp* regnal year

*ḥꜣtt* prow rope

*ẖr ḥꜣt* formerly

*ḥꜣt ib* grief, sadness

*ḥꜣt-sp* regnal year

*ḥꜣtyw* linen

*ḥꜣt-sp* regnal year

*ḥꜣd* fish trap, trap fish

*ḥꜣd* lust

*ḥi* *ḥip* hasten

*m-ḥis* to face someone (aggressively)

*ḥwi, ḥii* strike, beat, drive in, tread (a road), hit

**ḥy** *ḥwyt* rain

**ḥʿ** *ḥʿ* palace

*ḥʿ* piece of flesh, member

*ḥʿw* flesh, body, members

*ḥʿw* self

*ḥʿw-nṯr* the king (lit - flesh of the god)

*ḥʿi* rejoice, joyful

*ḥʿʿw* rejoice

*ḥʿʿwt* joy

*ḥʿwt* joy

*ḥʿȝ* child, lad, infant

*ḥʿȝw* children

*ḥʿw* ships

*ḥ(w)ʿw* short men

*ḥʿpy* inundation, (god) Hapi

*ḥʿpyw* inundations

*ḥʿt* wick

*ḥʿḏȝ* pillage, plunder, plunderer

**ḥw** *ḥw* royal decree

*ḥw* (god of Authoritative Utterance) Hu

*ḥw* food, sustenance

*ḥwȝ* to rot, decay

*ḥwy ȝ* Would that!

*ḥwʿ* short

*ḥ(w)ʿw* short men

*ḥwn* youthful, youth, vigor, be young, refreshed, child, yong man

*ḥwnt* maiden

***ḥw-ny-r-ḫr*** combat

***ḥwrw*** be poor, helpless, wretched, wretch

***ḥwrw*** wretch

***bw ḥwrw*** wretchedness, misery

***sḥwr*** vilify

***sḥwrw*** to abuse, vilify

***ḥwt*** house, temple, tomb, walled enclosure, district

***nbt-ḥwt*** (goddess) Nephtys

***ḥwt ꜥꜣt*** castle

***ḥwt-wꜥrt*** Avaris (LE) (Hyksos capital in the Nile Delta)

***ḥwt nṯr*** temple (lit - god's house)

***ḥwt ḥr*** (goddess) Hathor

***ḥwt kꜣ*** tomb chapel (lit - soul house)

***tp-ḥwt*** roof

***ḥwtf*** to rob, plunder

***ḥb*** ***ḥb*** catch (of game)

***ḥb*** feast, festival

***ḥby*** make a festival

***ḥbyt*** festival offerings

***ḥbw*** festivals

***ḥb sd*** **"Sed"** festival, jubilee

***ḥbt*** ritual book

***ḥb*** celebrate a triumph

***sḥb*** make festive, adorn

***ḥb [n]*** to mourn [for]

***ḥbꜥ*** play (a game)

*ḥbꜣbꜣ* waddle (of goose)

*ḥbw* target

*ḥbbt* water

*ḥbs* to bear (a ceremonial fan)

*ḥbs* to clothe, cover

*ḥbswt* cloth

*ḥbsw* clothing, clothes

*ẖry-ḥbt* lector priest

**ḥp** *ḥpy* (god) Hepy (son of Horis)

*ḥpw* Apis bull

*ḥp(wy)* (sunshade god) Hepuy

*ḥpwty* runner

*ḥpt* embrace

*ḥpt* oar

*[iti] [ḏsr] ḥpt* row (lit - take or ply the oar)

*ḥpt* go by boat

*ḥpt* boat

**ḥf** *ḥf* range (of game)

*ḥfꜣ w* snake, serpent

*ḥfꜣ t* crawling

*ḥfn, ḥfnw* 100,000

*ḥfnr* tadpole

**ḥm** *ḥm* assuredly, indeed

*ḥm* majesty (of king or god)

*ḥm* male slave

*ḥm nṯr* prophet, high priest

*ḥm kꜣ* "**ka**" priest

***ḥmt*** female slave

***ḥm3t*** salt

***ḥm3gt*** Nubian red stone

***ḥm(ỉ)*** flee, retire, retreat

***ḥm*** coward

***ḥm ḫt*** retreat

***ḥm*** steer

***ḥmw*** steering oar

***ḥmy*** helmsman

***ḥm3t*** salt

***ḥmw*** be skilled, skillful

***ḥmw*** be skilled, skillful

***ḥmw ỉb*** clever, skillful

***ḥmww*** craftsman

***ḥmwwtyw*** craftsmen

***ḥmwt*** craftsmen

***ḥmt*** craft, art

***ḥmwy*** work

***ḥmww*** washerman

***ḥmsỉ*** sit, sit down, dwell, besiege

***ỉḥms*** occupant (in titles)

***ˁḥˁ ḥmsỉ*** pass one's life

***ḥmsỉ ḥr*** beseige

***ḥmsw*** sloth

***ḥmst*** council (of the king and courtiers)

***ḥm3gt*** carnelian

***ḥmt*** craft, art

*ḥmt* majesty (of queen or goddess)

*ḥmt* target stand

*ḥmt* wife, woman

*iri ḥmt* take a wife

*ḥmt- nṯr* god's wife (queen's title)

*idt* vulva, cow

*ḥmt* copper, bronze

*ḥn* — *ḥn* go, depart

*ḥn* together with, and

*ḥn* provide, equip, command, govern

*ḥn* encumber, obstruct

*ḥn* control, occupy, command, commend, supply, equip

*ḥnw* commanders

*sḥn* to command

*ḥn* temple receptacle

*ḥnwt* horn

*ḥni* rush

*ḥnyt* spear

*ḥnꜥ, ḥn* together with, and

*ḥnꜥw* therewith, together with them

*ḥnw* vessel

*ḥnw* (god) Sokar's bark

*ḥnwt* mistress

*ḥnwty* servant

*ḥnbwt* confines (of area)

*ḥnmw* god Khnum

*ḥnmmt* sun people of Heliopolis, mankind

*ḥnn* hoe

***ḥnn*** phallus

***ḥnhn*** be detain, hinder

***ḥns*** be narrow

***ḥnsk*** tie up

***ḥnskt*** lock (of hair)

***ḥnk*** to present, offer

***ḥnkw*** gifts

***ḥnkt*** offerings

***ḥnkyt*** bed, couch

***ḥnḳt*** beer

***ḥnt*** occupation, craft

***ḥnt*** two (both) sides (of)

***ḥnt*** swampy lake

***ḥnt*** horn

***ḥnt*** cup

***ḥntꜣsw*** lizard

***ḥnt(y)*** be greedy, covetous

***ḥnty*** commander

***ḥnty*** horse attendant

***ḥnty*** period, end

***ḥr*** ***ḥr*** face, sight

***m ḥr f*** in his sight

***rdi m ḥr n [r]*** charge, command [to]

***ẖr st ḥr f*** under his supervision

***ḥr nb*** everyone

***ḥr*** upon, in at, from, on account of, through, and, having on it, because, from, after

***ꜣmi [ḥr]*** mix, compound [with]

*ꜣr [ḥr]* restrain, hold back [from], drive away, oppress

*inḏ ḥr* hail to

*ꜥḥꜥ ḥr* indulgent

*wn ḥr* instructed, expert

*wn ḥr n* enlightenment is given to

*[m] ḥry ib* in the midst of

*m ḥr f* in his sight

*mr ḥr ib n* be displeasing to

*mdw ḥr* speak to, litigate about

*r-ḥry* master chief

*rdi m ḥr n* charge, command (person)

*ḥr(y) ib* middle

*ḥs ḥr.f* courageous

*r ḥrw* up

*ḥms(i) ḥr* besiege

*ḥr -ꜥ* arrears, remainder

*ḥryw-rnpt* epagomenal days

*ḥry-ḫt-f* offering loaf

*ḥry-sꜣ* a breed of cattle

*ḥrw* upper part

*ḥr m* why

*ḥr ntt* because

*ḥr [r]* be far, distant [from]

*[ḥr] snw [sy]* [for] another [time]

*ḥrt* heaven, sky

*ḥrt* road

*ḥrt* hill-side tomb

*ḥr tp* chieftain, chief

*ḥrt-š* garden

*(r) ḫft ḥr* in front of, in the presence of

*sꜣwy ḥr* keep an eye on

*st-ḥr* supervision

*sḏꜣy ḥr* divert oneself, amuse oneself

*ḥry* who (which) is over, captain, commander, above, upper

*ḥry sštꜣ* "He who is over the secrets"

*ḥry (n) tm* an obscrue title

*tpt--ḥr(y)* master

*ḥr* (falcon god) Horus

*ḥr-ꜣḫty* Horus of the horizon, Horakhti

*ḥr-nḫny* (god) Horus of Hekhen

*ḥt-ḥr* (goddess) Hathor

*ḥr nbw* Golden Horus (king's title)

*ḥr* rope

*ḥr* prepare

*ḥr,* dread, terror, terrible

*ḥryt* dred, terror, respect

*ḥr(y) ib* middle

*ḥr [r]* be far, distant [from]

*[m] ḥr(y)-ib* [in] the midst of

*ḥr(y)-ib(y)* who dwells in (said of deities)

*ḥr [r]* be far, distant [from]

*ḥry* above, who is over, captain, head man

*ḥryw-šꜥy* Beduin

***ḥryt*** dread

***ḥry-tꜣ*** survivor

***ḥry-tp*** chief, chieftain, who is upon, who is over

***ḥr ꜥ, ḥr ꜥwy*** immediately

***ḥrw*** upper part

***r ḥrw*** up

***ḥrw r*** apart from, as well as, besides

***sḥr*** drive away, banish

***ḥrf*** kind of bread

***ḥr m*** why?

***ḥr nb*** everyone

***ḥr ntt*** because

***ḥr-r*** be far from, besides

***ḥrrt*** flower

***ḥrst*** carnelian

***ḥr gs*** beside, in the presence of

***dỉ ḥr gs*** dispose of, kill, show partiality

***ḥrt*** heaven, sky

***ḥrt*** road

***ḥrt*** tomb

***ḥrt*** hill-side tomb

***ḥrty*** travel (by land)

***ḥrt-ỉb*** central hall (of a temple)

***ḥr tp*** chieftain, chief

***ḥrtt*** piece of lapis

***m ḥry ỉb*** in the midst of

**ḥh** ***ḥh*** (god) Heh, one million, a great number

*ḥḥ n* many, countless

*ḥḥ* *nḥḥ* eternity, forever

*ḥḥy* seek, search for, be missing

*ḥs* *ḥs* freeze, be cold

*ḥs* turn back, turn homeward

*ḥs ḥr.f* courageous

*ḥs* excrement

*ḥsꜣt* sacred cow

*ḥsỉ* to praise, favor, sing, honor

*ḥsy* favored one, honored one

*ḥsw* singer

*ḥswt* praises, favors, honors

*ḥswtỉ* favorite

*ḥst* praise, favor, honor

*ḥsty* praise

*ḥsyt* concubine

*ḥsb* workman

*ḥsb* reckon, count

*ḥsb* break, smash, fracture

*ḥsb* 1/4, 1/4 aroura

*ḥsbw* doom

*ḥsp* garden

*ḥsmn* natron

*ḥsmn* bronze

*ḥsḳ* cut off, hew off

*ḥst* water pot

***ḥḳ*** *ḥḳꜣ* rule, govern

*ḥḳꜣ* ruler, governor, chieftain

*ḥḳꜣ* ruler, king

*ḥḳꜣ ḥwt* district governor, village chief

*ḥḳꜣt* scepter

*ḥḳꜣt* rulership

*ḥḳꜣt* **"hekat"** measure (4.5 liters)

*ḥḳr* be hungry, hunger

*ḥḳr* hungry man

*ḥḳt* (frog goddess) Heket

***ḥk*** *ḥkꜣ* magic

*ḥkn* exult, be joyful, acclaim

*ḥknw* exultation, praise, thanksgiving

*ḥkt* (frog goddess) Heket

***ḥt*** *ḥ(w)t* attack (of falcon)

*ḥtꜣw* sail

*ḥtyt* throat, wind pipe

*ḥtꜥ* bed

*ḥtw* bowls

*ḥtp* altar

*ḥtp* gift, boon

*ḥtp di nsw* a gift the king gives (offering formula)

*ḥtpt ḏf(ꜣ)* food offerings

*ḥtpt* cavern, snake hole

*ḥtptw* offerings

*ḥtp(w)-nṯr* divine offerings

*ḥtptw ḏf(ꜣ)* food offerings

***ḥtp*** be pleased, happy, gracious, at peace, calm, satisfied, at rest, content, pacify, occupy

***ḥtpw*** peace, contentment, submission

***sḥtp*** to please, satisfy, pacify, provide for

***ḥtpt*** bundle (of herbs)

***ḥtpt*** bowl (for bread offerings)

***ḥtpyw*** non-combatants

***ḥtm*** perish, be destroyed

***sḥtm*** destroy

***sḥtmw*** destroyer

***ḥtmt*** chair

***ḥtr*** assess, tax, levy, provide

***ḥtr*** team of horses, chariotry

***ḥtr*** team of oxen

***ḥts*** complete, end, celebrate (a feast)

***ḥtt*** mine, quarry

***ḥtt*** hyena

***ḥd***

***ḥdb*** throw down, be prostrate

***ḥdb [ḥr]*** sit, stop [at] (someplace)

***ḥḏ***

***ḥḏ*** mace

***ḥḏ*** white, be bright

***inr ḥḏ*** limestone

***ḥḏ*** white clothes

***ḥḏt*** white linen

***ḥḏt*** the white crown of Upper Egypt

***ḥḏ tꜣ*** dawn

***ḥḏ*** set forth at dawn

 ***ḥḏḏwt*** brightness

 ***sḥḏ*** to brighten, light up, illuminate, make clear

 ***sḥḏ*** instructor, inspector

 ***t ḥḏ*** white bread

 ***ḥḏ*** silver

 ***pr-ḥḏ*** treasury

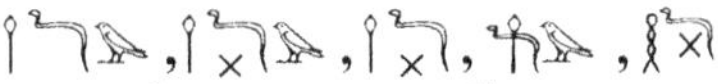 ***ḥḏỉ*** to damage, injure, disobey, destroy, upset eclipse, waste

 ***ḥḏw*** onions

 ***ḥḏn*** be vexed

# ḫ (sometimes replaced with h̲)

*ḫ* placenta

ḫꜣ *ḫꜣ* 1,000

*ḫꜣ* administrative office

*ḫꜣi* measure, examine (a patient)

*sḫꜣ [n]* remember, recall [to]

*ḫꜣy* plumb line

*ḫꜣyt* illness, disease

*ḫꜣyt* slaughter, massacre

*ḫꜣꜥ* throw, put, leave, desert

*ḫꜣw* bowl

*ḫ(ꜣ)w(y)* night, late evening

*ḫꜣw* plants

*ḫꜣw (nw sšn)* lotus plants

*ḫꜣwt* (animal) hide

*ḫꜣt, ḫꜣwt, ḫꜣ(y)t* table of offerings

*ḫꜣb* hippopotamus

*ḫꜣ bꜣ s* starry sky

*ḫꜣbb* crookedness

*ḫꜣbb* crookedness

*ḫꜣfꜥ* capture (in war), grasp

*ḫꜣmi* bend arm in respect, bow down , bend over

*ḫꜣmt ḫt* pile of offerings

*ḫꜣrw* Khor (in Canaan)

*ḫꜣrw* one from Khor

***ḫȝrt*** widow

***ḫȝḫ*** hasten, swift, hurry, quick of speech, impatient

***ḫȝrt, ḫȝrt*** widow

***ḫȝs*** scramble

***ḫȝs*** creek

***ḫȝst*** foreign land, hill country

***ḫȝstyw*** foreigners, desert dwellers

***ḫȝt*** swamp, marsh

***ḫȝty*** office

***ḫȝtb*** have pity

***ḫy*** ***ḫyš*** bundle (of vegetables)

***ḫꜥ*** ***ḫꜥ*** hill of the sunrise

***ḫꜥi*** appear, shine

***ḫꜥw*** weapons

***ḫꜥw*** crown

***ḫꜥw*** funeral furniture, weapons, equipment

***ḫꜥm*** approach, appear (with hostile intent)

***ḫꜥr*** to rage

***ḫw*** ***ḫwi*** to protect, exclude

***ḫw, ḫwt*** protection

***ḫw*** exclusion

***ḥr ḫw*** except

***wꜥ ḥr ḫw f*** unique

***ḫw*** fan

***ḫww*** evil, baseness

***ḫwsi*** pound , tamp, build, accomplish

***ḫw, ḫwt*** protection

***ḫwt*** sanctuary

***ḫwd*** rich

***sḫwd*** enrich

***ḫb*** ***ḫbꜣ*** destroy, overwhelm

***ḫbyt*** carnage, slaughter, destruction

***ḫbỉ*** dance

***ḫbwt*** (female) dancers

***ḫbỉ*** to lessen, subtract, deduct, distort, be guilty

***ḫbt*** deduction, exaction

***ḫbt*** place of execution

***ḫbn*** be guilty, distorted

***ḫbnt*** crime, accusation

***ḫbnt y*** criminal

***ḫbs*** hoe, cultivate

***ḫbsw*** cultivated lands

***ḫbst*** beard, tail

***ḫbstyw*** bearded ones of Punt

***ḫbt*** dance

***ḫbd*** to blame, disapprove of, be hateful

***ḫp*** ***ḫpỉ*** walk, encounter

***šḫpỉ*** bring

***ḫpyt*** death

***ḫpp*** strange

***ḫpn*** fat

***ḫpr*** come into existence, become, happen, make

***ḫprw*** form, shape, upbringing, stages of growth

*ḫprt* occurance

*ḫpr ḏs f* he who created himself

*sḫpr* create, bring to pass, train

*ḫpr* become

*ḫpri* (sun god at rising) Khepri

*ḫprr* dung beetle

*ḫprš* the blue crown

*ḫpš* foreleg, thigh, arm

*ḫpš* strong arm, strength, power

*m-ḫpš* acquire by one's own strength

*ḫpš* scimetar

*ḫpš* Great Bear constellation

*ḫpt* die, death, decease

*ḫpdw* buttocks

**ḫf**

*ḫfꜥ* seize, grip, grasp

*ḫfꜥ* a cake

*ḫfꜥt* food

*ḫft* in front of, as well as, corresponding to, in accordance with, when, according as, at the time of

*(r) ḫft ḥr* in front of, in the presence of

*r ḫft* in front of

*ḫft ntt* in view of the fact that

*ḫft(w)* accordingly

*ḫfty* enemy

*ḫftyw* enemies

**ḫm**

*ḫm* hot

*sḫmm* make warm

*ḫm* wild

*ḫm* be ignorant

*ḫm* ignorant man

*sḫm* forget

*i͗ḫm sk* indestructable

*ḫm* shrine

*ḫm* sacred image

*ḫm* be dry

*ḫmw* dust

*ḫm* Letopolis (Ausim) (in Delta)

*ḫmꜥt* oar handle

*ḫmnw* Hermopolis (Ashmunen) (UE)

*ḫmnyw* the 8 deities of Hermopolis

*ḫmntyw* special king of ship

*ḫmt* three, for a third time, treble

*ḫmt nw* third

*ḫmt rw* 3/4

*ḫmt* foretell, expect, think, intend, plan, anticipate

*ḫmt* the absence of, without

*smḫ* forget

*ḫtm* valuables

*ḫn* *ḫn* rebel

*ḫn* speech, sentence, utterance, matter, affair

*ḫni͗* alight, halt

*ḫni͗* restrain

*ḫnw* resting place, dwelling

*ḫnp* rob, despoil, offer

***ḫnm*** to smell , to give pleasure

***ḫnms*** friend, associate with

***ḫnmt*** red jasper, carnelian

***ḫnr*** restrain

***ḫnrwt*** women of the harem

***ḫnrw*** reins

***ḫnrtt*** conspiracy

***ḫns*** traverse

***ḫnsw*** the tenth month

***ḫnš*** stink

***ḫnwt*** female musician

***ḫnt*** festival expense

***ḫnt*** face

***ḫnt*** harim, prison, fortress

***ḫnt*** first, foremost, in front of, (go) forth, among, from

***imy ḫnt*** priestly title

***m ḫnt*** within, out of

***ḫnti*** sail (travel) southward

***ḫntit*** southward voyage

***sḫnti*** take southward

***ḫnti-ib*** glad of heart

***ḫnty*** who or what is in front of

***sḫnti*** advance, promote

***ḫnty*** crocodile

***ḫnty-ḫty*** the eleventh month

***ḫntyw*** tenants

***ḫntyw-tꜣ*** Southerners

***ḫntw*** racks for water pots

*ḫnt-ḥn-nfr* Nubian region south of the second cataract

*ḫntš* walk about

*ḫntš* wooded country, garden

*ḫntš [m] [ḫr]* take pleasure [in]

*ḫnd* tread

*ḫnd* lower part, calf (of leg)

**ḫr**

*ḫr* under (king), with, near, to, by, and, further

*ḫr* fall, defeated

*ḫrw* (defeated) enemy

*sḫr(t)* overthrow, defeat

*ḫr* and, further

*ḫrw* voice, cry

*prt-ḫrw* voice (or votive) offering

*ḫrw fy* he says

*ḫrw* low lying land

*ḫrwy* enemy

*ḫrp* district, estate

*ḫrp* baton of office

*ḫrp* at the head, in front, control, administer, undertake, make an offering of

*ḫrp* director, leader

*ḫrp nsty* controller of the two seats

*ḫrp k3t* controller of works, builder, architect

*ḫrp k3t* to start works or constructions

*ḫrpw* mallet

*ḫrš* bundle (of vegetables)

*ḫrt* state, condition, requirements, products

*ḫrt-ib* wish, desire

**ḫḫ** *ḫḫ* throat

**ḫs** , *ḫsy* bribe

*ḫsbd* lapis lazuli

, *ḫsf* spin

, , , *ḫsf* repel, oppose, punish

*ḫsf-ꜥ* oppose, opposition

() () , () , , *ḫsfi* travel upstream, southward

*ḫm* shrine

*ḫm* Letopolis (Ausim) (in Delta)

, *ḫsr ḫsr* ward off, drive away, clear, dispel

**ḫt** *ḫt* accompaning, after

() *imy ḫt* who follows, accompanies, bodyguard, attendant

() , () *m ḫt* after, afterward, accompanying

*ḫt* throughout, pervading

( ) *ḫt (ḫt)* throughout, pervading

*ḫtḫt* throughout

*ḫti* retire, retreat

*ḫtḫt* be reversed, retreat

*ḫt* wood, timber, tree, woodland

, *ḫt tꜣw, ḫt* mast

*r ḫt* under the authority of (lit- under the mast)

, *ḫt* Hatti, land of the Hittite

*ḫt* fire

, , *ḫt, iḫt* thing(s), something, anything, matter, affair

()(), *ḫti* to carve, sculpture

()() *ḫtyw* threshing floor

*ḫtyw* terrace, terraced hill, platform, dais

*ḫt-ꜥꜣ* poultry, edible fowl

*ḫtwt* furniture

*ḫt* throughout, pervading, through

*ḫft* in front of, as well as, corresponding to, in accordance with, when, according as, at the time of

*ḫtm* chest, storehouse

*ḫtm* to shut, close, seal

*ḫtmt* contract

*ḫtḫt* through

*ḫt ṯꜣw* mast

**ḫd**

*ḫdi* sailing downstream, travel north

*m-ḫdi* northward

*ḫdt* land register

# ẖ (sometimes replaced with ḫ)

***ẖt*** body, belly

***ẖwt*** bodies, bellies

**ẖꜣ** ***ẖꜣyt*** pile of corpses

***ẖꜣb*** sickle

***ẖꜣbt*** curly appendage (on crown)

***ẖꜣbb*** crookedness

***ẖꜣbt*** curly appendage (on crown)

***ẖꜣmi, ẖꜣmi*** bow down, bend over

***ẖꜣmt ẖt, ẖꜣmt ẖt*** pile of offerings

***ẖꜣr*** sack, a large measure of capacity

***ẖꜣrt*** widow

***ẖꜣẖti*** tempest

***ẖꜣkw ib*** disaffected, rebellious, rebel

***ẖꜣt*** oxyrhynchus fish

***ẖꜣt*** quarry, mine

***ẖꜣt, ẖꜣt*** swamp, marsh

***ẖꜣt*** corpse

***ẖꜣyt*** pile of corpses

***ẖꜣt*** table of offerings

**ẖꜥ** ***ẖꜥm, ẖꜥm*** approach with hostile intent)

***ẖꜥḳ*** shave

***ẖꜥḳw*** barber

**ẖp** ***ẖpꜣ*** navel, umbilical

***ẖpw*** sculptured reliefs

***ẖpn*** fat

**ẖm** *ẖms* bend (one's back), bow

**ẖn** *ẖn* approach, draw near

*ẖn* tent

*ẖni* to row, convey (by boat)

*ẖnyt* sailors

*ẖnw* sailor

*ẖnt* procession (by water)

*mẖnt* ferry boat

*mẖnty* ferry boat operator

*ẖnw* interior

*ʿẖnwty* inner chambers, audience hall

*[m]-ẖnw* [in the] interior, inside

*ẖnw* royal residence

*ẖnw* stream, brook

*ẖnw-ʿwy* embrace

*ẖnwtyw* skin clad people

*ẖnm* herd

*ẖnm [m]* join, unite, become joined [with]

*ẖnmw* house mates, associates

*ẖnmw* (god) Khnum

*ẖnm(t)* nurse

*ẖnmt* well, cistern, water source

*ẖnn* destroy, interfere, disturb

*ẖnnw* turmoil, uproar

*sẖn* demolish (a wall)

*ẖnt* skin

***ẖnwtyw*** skin clad people

***ẖnt*** burial chamber

***ẖnty*** statue, image

***ẖr***

***ẖr*** under, carrying, holding, at, possessing

***bw ẖry f*** the place where is (lit - the place under him)

***[m] [r] [ẖr] ḥȝt*** in front of, before

***[m] ḥr m ẖrw*** [with] face downcast

***ẖr ʿ*** in the charge of

***ẖry*** which is under, lower

***ẖry ʿ*** subordinate, assistant

***ẖry-ḥbt*** lector priest

***ẖrw*** base, lower part, under side

***ẖr ḥȝt*** in front of, before, formerly

***ẖr(t)-nṯr*** necropolis

***ẖr st ḥr f*** under his supervision

***ẖrt*** possessions, belongings, portion, due, duty

***ẖrtyw-nṯr*** necropolis workmen

***ẖrt-hrw*** daytime, daily

***ẖrw*** kinfolk

***ẖrwy*** testicles

***ẖrd*** child

***ẖrdw*** childhood

***ẖrdt*** children

***ẖs***

***ẖsy*** weak, feeble, vile

***ẖsyt*** wrongdoing

***ẖsr ẖsr*** ward off, drive away, clear, dispel

***ẖḳ***

***ẖḳs*** be injured

**ẖk** — ***ẖkr*** be adorned

- ***ẖkrt*** concubine, hairdresser
- ***ẖkryt nsw*** king's ornament (concubine title)
- ***ẖkrw*** ornament, insignia
- ***sẖkr*** adorn

**ẖt** — ***ẖt*** body, belly

- ***n ẖt.f*** of his body

***ẖt*** body of people, generation

***ẖtb*** overthrow, kill

**ẖd** — ***ẖdb*** kill

**S** *s -* (causative prefix)

*s* she, her, it, its

*s* door bolt

*s* man

*s* gold vessel

*s* sheaf (for arrows)

*sȝ* *sȝ* barn

*sȝ* protection

*sȝ* weak

*s(i)* go!

*s(i)* man, someone, anyone, person

*s nb* everyone

*sȝ* son

*sȝt* daughter

*sȝ rꜥ* son of Ra (the king)

*sn* they, them, their

*st* it, them

*st, st ḥmt* woman

*sȝ* animal hobble, protection

*sȝ* company, regiment (of troops)

*sȝ* **protection**

*sȝ* 1/8 aroura (land measure)

*sȝ* back

*(m)(r)(ḥr) sȝ* after

*rdi sȝ [r]* flee, put a stop [to]

*sȝ* cattle pen, door, outside

***sꜣi*** be satiated, sated, be wise, understanding

***ssꜣi*** feed, sate

***rdi ib m-sꜣ*** be anxious about

***ssꜣi*** satisfy, enwisen

***sꜣi*** linger, lag

***sꜣw*** to guard, protect, ward off, restrain, beware lest

***sꜣw*** guardian, warden

***sꜣw*** beam, plank

***sꜣw*** el Hagar (Sais) (LE)

***sꜣw*** to guard

***sꜣwi*** lengthen, prolong

***sꜣwy ḥr*** keep an eye on

***sꜣwi ib*** to gladden (lit - to lengthen the heart)

***sꜣwy*** 2/3

***sꜣwy*** 2/3 fine gold

***sꜣwy ḥr*** keep an eye on

***sꜣwt*** stand guard against, watch

***sꜣwty*** guardian

***sꜣwt*** Asyut (UE)

***sꜣwt*** walls

***sꜣb*** cause to delay

***sꜣb*** cross (water)

***sꜣb*** jackal

***sꜣb*** dignitary, worthy

***sꜣb*** cross (water)

***sꜣb*** variegated, dappled

***sꜣb šwt*** variegated of feathers (of Horus)

*sȝbt* dappled cow

*sȝm* cause to burn, burn up

*sȝmt* mourning

*sȝr* need, requirement

*sȝirw* need

*sȝr* needy one

*sȝr* be wise

*sȝrt* wisdom, understanding

*sȝḥ* dependant

*sȝḥ* grant, endowment

*sȝḥ* land grant

*sȝḥ* toe

*sȝḥ* (constellation) Orion

*sȝḥ* approach, reach, arrive at, kick

*sȝḥw* neighbors, dependants

*[m] sȝḥt* [in] the neighborhood

*sȝẖ* glorify *sȝsȝ* to force, repel

*sȝḳ* collect, gather together

*sȝt* wall

*sȝty-bity* the royal twins, Shu & Tefnet

*sȝty-gb* "son of Geb"

*sȝsȝ* repel, force (boat), overthrow

*sȝḳ [r]* collect, gather together, gird [against]

*sȝt* wall

*sȝtw* ground, earth, floor

*sȝtw* floor

**sỉ** *sỉ* go!

*sỉ, sbỉ* perish

*sỉꜣ* recognize, perceive

*sỉꜣ* (god of perception) Sia

*sỉꜣt* piece of cloth

*sỉꜣt* purloin, cheat

*sỉꜣty* cheat

*sỉw [r]* bring a complaint [against]

*sỉwḥ* inundate

*sỉwḫ* rob

*sỉp* revise, inspect, assign, examine, destine, organize

*sỉpty* revision, inspect, investigation

*sỉmꜣ* make well disposed

*sỉn* to smear

*sỉn* clay, plaster

*sỉnt* clay seal

*sỉn* delay, hasten, die

*sỉnw* runners

*sỉnw* ropes

*sỉnt* canoe

*sỉḳr* advance, promote (a person), adorn (a place)

**sy** *sy* she, her, it its

*sy* who?, what?, which?

**sꜥ** *sꜥꜣy* make great, glorify

*sꜥꜣy* tremble

*sꜥb* to cut out, to castrate

*sꜥb* be equiped

***sꜥm*** to swallow down, wash down (food)

***sꜥnḫ*** make to live, preserve, nurish

***sꜥnd*** to dimish

***sꜥr*** make to ascend, offer up

***sꜥry*** basin on a stand

***sꜥryt*** uraeus

***sꜥrḳ*** finish, complete, put an end to

***sꜥrḳ*** kill

***sꜥḥ*** mummy

***sꜥḥ*** be noble, rank, dignity, nobleman, worthy

***sꜥḥ*** royal rank

***sꜥḥ*** to ennoble

***sꜥḥ*** (deceased) noble

***sꜥḥꜥ*** to erect (an oberisk, etc)

***sꜥšꜣ*** multiply

***sꜥḳ*** cause to enter

***sꜥḳ-nṯr*** god's entry

***sꜥḳꜣ*** set or put in order

***sw*** ***sw*** day (in dates)

***sww*** dates, particular days

***sw, swt*** he, him, it, his, its, (rarely) she

***swꜣ*** cut off, cut down

***swꜣ*** pass by, escape, surpass, pass away, remove, transgress, occur, journey

***swꜣḥ*** cause to endure

***swꜣš*** extol, applaud, pay honor to

***swꜣi*** pass by, escape, surpass, pass away, remove, transgress, occur

***sw(ꜣ)d*** renew, make green, make flourish, hand over, bequeath

***swꜥb*** purify, cleanse

***swbꜣ*** open

***swmnw*** Sumenu

***swmt*** make thick

***swn*** to barter

***swnt*** sale, barter, exchange

***swn*** perish

***sswn*** destroy, destruction

***swnw*** physician

***swnt*** arrow

***swnt*** price

***swr*** promote, increase

***swr*** to drink

***swrỉ*** drink

***swh [n]*** to boast [about]

***swhn*** tear down

***swḥt*** egg

***swḫꜣy*** decay

***swsr*** make powerful

***swsẖ*** widen, extend, enlarge

***swt*** but, he, it, she

***swt*** breeze

***swt*** sedge plant

***swt*** leg of beef, tibia

***swtwt*** promenade, walk around, journey

***swdi*** to plant

***swḏ*** hand over, assign

***swḏȝ*** make healthy, keep safe

**sb** ***sbȝ*** star

***sbȝ [r]*** teach [about]

***sbȝ*** door, entrance

***sbȝ*** to teach

***sbȝyt*** teachings, instructions

***sbi*** perish, be faint

***sbi*** go, pass, send, attain, conduct, load

***sbi*** drink

***sbi*** go, travel. conduct, spend (time), attain

***sbi*** to rebel

***sbi*** rebel

***sbi*** rebel serpent

***sbit*** rebels

***sbw*** spoils (of war)

***sbn*** slip, go astray

***sbhȝ*** cause to retreat

***sbḥ*** cry aloud, cry

***sbẖ*** to wall in, enclose, shut away

***sbẖt*** gateway, portal

***sbẖt*** pylon-shaped chest

***sbḳ*** leg, calf, splendid, precious

***sbḳ*** excellent, successful

***sbk*** (god) Sobek

***sbt*** laugh, laughter, mirth

*sbt* wrong, evil

*sbt* libation jar

*sbty* surrounding wall, rampart

*sbtw* in search of

*sp* — *sp* time, occasion, happen

*n sp* together, at once

*sp-sn* two times (repeat previous word)

*ḥꜣt-sp* regnal year

*r tnw sp* every time that

*spꜣ* centipede

*spꜣt* district, nome

*spỉ* remain over, be left out, excluded, abondoned,be left over

*spyt* remainder, remnant

*spw* fragments

*spw* bundles of wood

*spr* rib

*spr* approach, arrive, reach

*sprt* to petition, appeal to

*sprt* petition

*sprw* petitions

*sprw, sprty* petitioner

*sprỉ* cause to miss, expel

*spḥ* attain

*spḥ* to lasso

*spḥw* lasso

*spḥt* ribs of beef

*spẖr* write out, copy

*spẖr* register, copy

***spẖr*** circulate

***spt*** threshing floor

***spt*** lip, border (of pool, etc)

***spt*** shore

***spt*** side edge of a boat

***spty*** lips

***spt*** ritual object

***spd*** sharp

***sspd*** make ready, supply

***spdw*** (god) Sopd

***spdt*** (dog star) Sirius (Sothis)

***spdd*** supply

*sf* ***sf*** mix

***sf*** yesterday

***sf*** be mild

***sfw*** muddle

***sfn*** be gentle, kind

***sfḫ*** unloose, take off (clothing)

***sfḫw*** seven

***sfḫt-ꜥbw*** "The seven Horned"

***sft*** sword, knife, slaughter, slaughterer

***sftw*** butcher

***sft*** anointing oil

***sft*** sacrifice

*sm* ***sm, stm*** "**Sem**" priest

***sm*** herb, plant

***sm*** succor, tend, occupation, pastime, event

*smꜣ* lung

*smꜣ* unite

*smꜣt* union

*smꜣ* scalp, locks of hair

*smꜣ* kill, destroy, smite, slay

*smꜣ* fighting bull

*smꜣ* priest who clothes the god

*smꜣyt* consort

*smꜣyt* association, confederation

*smꜣꜥ* to offer, put in order, survey

*smꜣꜥ ḫrw [r]* triumph [over]

*smꜣwy* renew, renovate

*smꜣr* afflict, harm

*smꜣt-ꜥ* an offering

*smꜣt-ꜥꜣt* a fabric

*smi* to report, announce, proclaim, acknowledgement

*smi* to chastise

*smi* lash, whip

*smyt* desert, necropolis

*smꜥ* Upper Egyptian corn

*smw* pastures

*smwn* probably, surely

*smn* kind of goose

*smn* preserve, record, make firm, fortify

*smn* establish

*smn* press down (bread)

*smnw* supports

***smnmn*** shift

***smnḫ*** advance, endow, confirm, restore

***smntyw*** emissaries

***smr*** courtier, friend

***smrw*** courtiers

***smḥ*** a light boat, skiff

***smḫ*** forget

***smsi*** deliver (a baby)

***smsw*** eldest

***smsw hyt*** elder of the portal

***smt*** desert, necropolis

***smt*** cloth (?)

***smtr*** bear witness to, examine, inquire

***smdt*** subordinates, staff, subjects

***sn*** — ***sn*** brother

***snt*** sister

***sn*** to smell, kiss

***sn*** to open

***sn*** reveal

***sn*** them, their, they

***sny*** those two, they two

***sni*** cut off

***sni*** to surpass, pass by

***sny mnt*** distress, calamity

***snʿʿ*** made smooth, ground fine

***snʿḥw*** angler, fisherman

***snw*** food offerings, food

***snw*** companion, equal

***snw*** pot

***snw*** two

***snnw*** second

***[ḥr] snw [sy]*** [for] another [time]

***snb*** health, healthy

***ssnb*** preserve

***s nb*** everyone, each

***snb*** overstep, overthrow

***snbb*** exchange greetings, converse

***snb ib*** famine

***snb*** leap over (a wall)

***snbt*** wall

***snbt*** jar

***snf*** last year

***snf*** make to breathe, succor, unload (a boat), empty out (contents), relieve, release

***snf*** blood

***snfr*** make perfect, make beautiful, embelish

***snm*** to feed (someone), feed on, eat, supply

***snm*** greed

***snmw*** food supply

***snm*** to be sad, grief

***snm*** torrential rain

***snm [n] [m]*** to pray [to], to beg [of]

***snn*** deed, title, copy, document

***snn*** image, portrait

***snnt*** likeness

***snny*** chariot soldier

***snr*** take care of

***snr*** terrify

***snhy*** to record, muster (troops)

***snhp*** spur on, start

***snḥ*** bind

***snḥm*** locust, grasshopper

***snẖn*** to nurse

***snẖn*** to control

***snẖt*** to strengthen

***snsy*** to praise, adore, worship

***snsw*** worship

***snsn*** fraternize, associate

***snḳ*** suckle

***snk*** tongue

***snk-ib*** haughtiness

***snkt*** darkness

***snktkt*** gossip

***snt*** flagstaff

***snwt*** flagstaffs

***snt*** sister

***snt*** (statue) base block

***snt*** feast of the sixth day

***snt*** likeness

***m snt r*** in the likeness of, in accordance with

***snty*** image, duplicate

***snṯ*** plan, plot out, found

***sntt*** ground plan, foundation

***snṯr*** incense

***snṯr*** cense, consecrate

***snḏ,*** fear

***snḏw*** fearful, timid or freightened man

***snḏt*** fear

***snḏm*** make happy, ease

***snḏm*** sit

***sr*** — ***sr*** a type of goose

***sr*** sheep, ram

***sr*** foretell, make known

***sr*** official, noble

***srwt*** office, magistracy

***sr-ꜥḥꜣ*** challenge to battle

***sryt*** military standard

***srwḫ*** tend (a patient), cherish

***srwt*** body of magistrates

***srwt*** prophecies

***srf*** temperature, warm, warmth, passion

***srf*** rest, repose

***srḫ*** banner (for the Horus name)

***srḫ*** complain, accuse

***srḫ*** learn about

***srḫ*** guilty one

***srs*** awaken, assume command

***srk*** relieve, admit breath to

***srḳt*** (goddess) Serket

***srt*** thorn

***srd*** glean

***srd*** to grow, to erect

***srd*** to plant

**sh** ***shꜣ*** confusion, disorder, lawlessness

***shꜣi*** send down, cause to fall

***shrỉ*** make content, bring peace

**sḥ** ***sḥ*** booth, arbor, council chamber

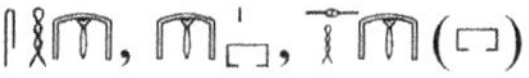

***sḥ*** counsel

***sḥ-nṯr*** divine booth, shrine of Anubis

***sḥwy*** collect, assemble, ~~assemblage~~

***sḥwy*** assemblage, collection

***sḥwr*** vilify

***sḥb*** make festive, adorn

***sḥm*** to stop (an act)

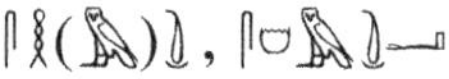

***sḥm*** pound, crush

***sḥn*** to command

***sḥn*** decorate

***sḥri*** drive away, banish

***sḥr*** fly

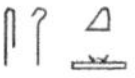

***sḥkꜣ*** cause to rule

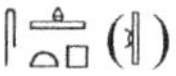

***sḥtp*** that pleases, that satisfies

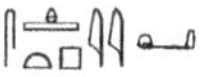

***sḥtpy*** censer

***sḥḏ*** inspector

**sẖ** ***sẖ*** to beat

***sẖt*** blow

***sḫw*** width

***sḫt*** marshland, country

***sḫt*** the marsh goddess

***sḫty*** peasant, fowler

***sḫtyw*** class of cattle

***sḫꜣ*** remember, recall

***sḫꜣw*** remembrance, memory

***sḫꜣw*** remembrance, memory, memorial

***sḫwy*** slaughter-house

***sḫwn*** dispute

***sḫws*** make prosperous

***sḫwd*** enrich

***sḫm*** sistrum, scepter

***sḫm*** "**sekhem**" scepter

***sḫm [m]*** have power [over], powerful, power

***sḫm ir f*** potentate

***sḫm*** forget

***sḫmm*** make warm

***sḫmḫ ib*** recreation, sport (lit - distract the heart)

***sḫmt*** power

***sḫmt*** (goddess) Sekhmet)

***sḫmty*** double crown

***sḫni*** alight

***sḫnt*** post, support (of heaven)

***sḫnti*** advance, promote

***sḫnti*** take southward

*sḫr* plan, counsel, determination, governance, conduct, condition, fortune, affair, fashion, nature, custom

*sḫry* captain, governor

*sḫr* overthrow, force into place

*sḫrt* papyrus roll

*sḫs* to run, hurry

*sḫsḫ* to run fast

*sḫt* trap, snare (birds), weave, make, form

*sḫt* stone patch

*sḫty* run

*sḫd* upside down, head down

*sẖ* — *sẖ, sḫ* be deaf

*sẖ ḥr [r]* turn a deaf ear [to]

*sẖꜣk* strain, empty completely

*sẖỉ* be deaf

*sẖꜥt* hare

*sẖb, sẖp* to swallow

*sẖm* to exert oneself, act violently, cope with

*sẖn* demolish (a wall)

*sẖnn, sẖnn* demolish (a wall)

*sẖr* to milk

*sẖr [m]* cover, coat, overlay [with]

*sẖrw* a linen fabric

*sẖkr* adorn

*ss* — *ssꜣỉ* satisfy, enwisen

*ssꜣw* provisions, sustenance

*sswn* destroy, destruction

***sswt*** metal inlay

***ssbḳ*** honor

***sspd*** make ready, supply

***ssfw*** garments

***ssm(t)*** horse

***ssn*** breathe

***ssnb*** preserve

***ssnt*** breathe

***ssnt*** to breathe

***ssnḏm*** a type of wood or tree

***srd*** to plant

***ssḥ*** smash, destroy

***sš***

***sš*** bird pool, nest

***sš*** spread out, pass

***sšy*** nest

***sš*** marsh

***sš*** to write, draw, paint, writing, book, letter

***sš*** scribe

***sšꜣt, sšt*** (goddess of writing) Seshat

***sšw*** writings

***sš wdḥw*** scribe of the offering table

***sš-šꜥt*** secretary

***sšꜣ*** prayer

***sšꜣy [n]*** pray [to], supplication

***sšꜣt, sšt*** (goddess) Seshat

***sšw*** metal ring or disk

***sšw*** to lose

***šsp, sšp*** daylight, white, dawn

***sšp*** receive, accept, take, catch

***sšm*** guide, lead, show, conduct

***iry sšm*** functionary

***sšm*** guidance, scheme, state of affairs

***sšmw*** divine shape, form, statue

***sšmw*** leader, ruler

***sšmt*** guiding serpent

***sšm*** butcher

***sšn, sššn*** lotus

***sšn*** lotus shaped cup

***sšnw*** ropes

***sšr*** recount, announce, discuss

***šsr*** arrow

***šsr, šs*** corn

***sšr, šs*** thing, concern, action

***mi sšr*** in good condition

***sšr*** linen

***sšrw*** linen (cloth) bag

***sšrw*** things, concerns, actions

***sššt*** sistrum

***sštꜣ*** mysterious, difficult, secret

***sštꜣw*** secretly

***sšd*** head band, bandage

***sšd*** don a head band

***sšd*** gleam, glitter, flash

***sšd*** lightning flash

***sšdw*** water drops

**sḳ**

*sḳꜣ* shrine base

*sḳꜣi* raise, prolong, set right

*sḳb* double

*sḳr* smite

*sḳr* captive

*sḳr-ꜥnḫ* captive

*sḳsn* make miserable

*sḳd* cause to build

*sḳdy* sail, travel by water

*sḳdi* sailor, traveler, sail

*sḳdw* sailor, traveler

*sḳdwt* sailing

*sḳdwt* company of troops

**sk**

*sk* Lo!

*sk* wipe, sweep,wipe out, pour out

*skꜣ* to plow

*skꜣt* cultivated land

*ski* perish, destroy

*sksk* destroy

*ski* pass (time)

*sky* accusation

*skw* battle, troops

*skm* grey haired

*skn [r]* be greedy, lust [after]

*skr* (god) Sokar

*sktw* kind of boat

*sktt* bark of the evening

*sg*

*sgmḥ* cause to see, glimpse

*sgnn* soften, weaken

*sgr* quiet

*sgrḥ* pacify, make peaceful

*st*

*st* pintail duck

*st* it, them, they

*st, st ḥmt* woman

*st* seat, place, throne

*st-ib* affection (lit - place in the heart)

*st-ns* speech

*st-r* occasion for speech, authority

*st-rd* rank

*st-ḥr* supervision

*ipt-swt* Karnak

*ꜣst* (goddess) Isis

*wsir* (god) Osiris

*st, sꜣt* pintail duck

*stꜣ, stꜣ* drag, draw, flow

*sti* successor

*st(i)* to pour

*st(i)* to stare at

*st(i) [r]* to shoot [at], throw, thrust [into], spear

*stw* target

*sti [m]* to kindle, set fire [to]

*sṯi, sṯt, sti* engender, beget

*styt* procreation, seed, posterity

*sṯi, sty, sṯ* perfume, odor

*sty r* breakfast time

? *sti*

*tꜣ-st(i)* Nubia

*styw* Nubians

*sty* a Nubian mineral

*sty* perfume

*styw* Asiatics

*stwt* rays

*stwt* resemble, even out, praise

*sṯni, stni* distinguish honor

*stp* cut up, choose, pick, cut off

*stp* dismembered, ruined

*stpt* choice

*stp* strip (of cloth)

*stp-sꜣ* protect, escort

*stp-sꜣ* palace

*sm, stm* "**Sem**" priest

*stny* to crown

*stnm* lead astray

*st ḥmt* woman

*stḥn* make dazzling

*stẖ stš* (god) Seth

*stkn* cause to approach, bring on

*stt* (godess) Satis

*stt* successor (female)

*stt, sṯt* Asia, Sehel Island (by Aswan, UE)

**sṯ**

*sṯ* Lo!, behold, now

*sṯ* scatter

*s(ꜣ)ṯ* libation stone

*sṯꜣ* a measure of capacity

*sṯꜣ* drag, draw, flow

*sṯꜣw* draging

*sṯꜣw* injury

*sṯꜣw*

*r-sṯꜣw* necropolis (of god Sokar)

*sṯꜣt* aroura (about 2/3 of an acre)

*sṯi, sṯy* perfume, odor

*sṯi, sṯt, sti* engender, beget

*sṯp* leap up, over leap

*sṯny* distinguish, honor

*sṯs* staff

*sṯsw* support, supporting

*sṯsy* be stretched out, prostrate

*sṯsy* upside down

*sṯt* beer jar

*stt, sṯt* Asia, Sehel Island (by Aswan, UE)

*sttyw* Asiatics

*sṯi, sṯt, sti* engender, beget

**sd**

*sd [m]* be clothed [in]

*sd* jubilee

*ḥb sd* "**Sed**" festival

*sd* tail

*sdty* a title (unknown meaning)

***sdȝ*** egret bird

***sdȝ*** tremble

***sdȝdȝ*** tremble

***sḏi*** to break

***sdwẖ*** treat, embalm

***sdb*** to swallow

***sḏb, sdb*** hinderance, obstacle, harm

***sdm*** to paint (the eyes)

***msdmt, msḏmt*** kohl, black eye paint

***sdm*** eye paint

***sdmi*** attach, annex

***sdni*** punish

***sdḥ*** bring down,, humiliate

***sdẖ*** well

***sdẖ*** hide, hide

***sdgȝ [r]*** hide or conceal [from]

***sdg*** hidden place

***sdgw*** hidden things

***sḏ*** ***sḏ*** break into, invade

***sḏȝ*** advisor

***sḏȝ*** go, pass by, die

***sḏȝy ḥr*** divert oneself, amuse oneself

***sḏȝyt*** seal

***sḏȝw*** rings

***sḏȝw*** precious

***sḏȝwty*** treasurer

***ns-sḏȝwty*** chief treasurer

***sḏꜣwtyw*** treasurers

***sḏꜣwty bity*** treasurer of King of Lower Egypt

***sḏ(i)*** to break

***sḏꜣmt*** pick

***sḏb, sdb*** hinderance, obstacle

***sḏwy*** slander

***sḏb, sdb*** hinderance, obstacle, harm

***sḏfꜣy*** endow, provide for

***sḏm*** to hear, obey

***sḏmi̓*** judge

***sḏm ꜥš*** servant

***sḏmt ꜥš*** female servant

***sḏr*** lie, spend the night, sleeping

***sḏr*** lie prostrate

***sḏr*** department

***sḏsr*** consecrate

***sḏt*** fire, flame

***sḏty*** child, foster child

***sḏd*** make permanent

***sḏd*** relate, tell

***sḏdt*** description

***sḏdw*** stories

## **Š** (sometimes replaced with s)

*š* pool, lake

*tꜣ š* the Fayyum (lit - lake land)

*šꜣ* — *šꜣ* marsh, meadow, countryside, lotus pool

*šꜣ* appoint, command, order, ordain, assign, settle, decide

*šꜣw* fate, destiny

*šꜣi, šꜣw* pig

*šꜣyt* fees, taxes

*šꜣꜥ* begin, be first, spring, originate, beginning

*šꜣꜥ m* beginning from

*(r) šꜣꜥ r* as far as, down to

*šwbty* ushabti figure

*šꜣbw* food, meals

*šꜣmw* soiled linen

*šꜣrḥꜣn* Sharahan (border town between Egypt and Palestine)

*šꜣs* travel

*šꜣs ḥtp* Shutb (Hypselis) (UE)

*šꜣsw* Shasu (desert northeast of Egypt)

*šꜣsw* Beduin of Shasu

*šꜣk* bag

*šꜣt* the land of Shat (south of Egypt)

*šꜣty* complement (of ship)

*šꜣd* to draw forth, rescue, educate, dig, dig out

*šꜥ* — *šꜥ* cut off, chop off

*šꜥt* slaughter, ferocity, blood lust

*šꜥd* cut down, cut off, cut up

*šꜥy* sand

*šꜥt* dispatch, letter

*sš-šꜥt* secretary

*šꜥty* 1/12 deben (about 1/4 oz)

*šꜥd* cut down, cut off, cut up

**šw** *šw* (air god) Shu

*šw* empty

*šw* blank papyrus

*šw* sun, sun light

*šw* be dry

*šwꜣ* be poor

*šwꜣ* poor man

*sšwꜣ* impoverish, deprive

*šwꜣb* persea tree

*šwꜣbty* "**ushabti**" funerary figure

*šwỉ [m]* be empty, free, devoid, missing [of, from]

*šwyt* shadow, shade

*šwyt* spirit, shade

*šwyt* god's image

*šww* a herb, a gourd

*šwb* persea tree

*šwbty* a jar

*šwt* neighbors

*šwt* feather

***šwty*** double plumes

***šwt*** shade, shadow

***šb*** ***šbi*** to change, alter, mix, mingle, confuse

***šbw*** food, meals

***šbb*** knead

***šbn [ḥr]*** mixed [with]

***šbnw*** various

***šbšb*** regulate, transform, adjust, divide

***šbt*** exchange

***šp*** ***šp*** be blind

***špnt*** beer measure

***špsi*** be noble, rich

***šps*** noble, revered (person), splendid (thing)

***šps*** noble (act)

***špss*** noble, august,esteemed

***špssw*** riches, wealth

***špt [r]*** be discontented [with]

***šf*** ***šfyt*** worth, dignity, majesty

***šfšfyt*** dignity

***šfšft*** ram's head, respect, awe

***šft*** ram headed figure (Amun)

***šfꜥ*** flight

***šfw*** to swell

***šf-tbt*** the sixth month

***šfdw*** papyrus (roll), register

***šfdw*** a ritual object

**šm** — *šm* go, depart

*šm* hot

*šm(ꜣ)w* wanderers, strangers, foreigners

*šmꜥ* barley from Upper Egypt

*šmꜥ* make music

*šmꜥyt* chantress

*šmꜥ(w)* Upper Egypt)

*šmꜥw iwnw* Thebes (UE) (lit - Heliopolis of Upper Egypt)

*wr mḏw šmꜥ(w)* "Greatest of the tens of Upper Egypt"

*šmꜥ* Upper Egyptian corn

*šmꜥ-s* White crown of Upper Egypt

*šmw* summer season

*šmw* harvest

*šmm* hot

*sšmm* heat

*šms* follow, accompany

*šmsw* follower

*šmsw* following, suite

*šmswt* following, suite

*šms wḏꜣ* funeral procession

**šn** — *šn* tree

*šn* ring

*šni* suffer

*šni* ask about

*šni* put down (strife)

*šni* exorcise, conjure

*šnt* enchantment, spell

*šn(i)* encircle, surround, enclose, cover

*šnw* circuit, circumference, enclosure, cartouche

*šnw* network, net

*šnw* eternity, 10,000,000, cartouche

*šn wr* the Ocean (lit - the great surround)

*šnyt, šnwt* courtiers

*šny* hair

*šnyt* rain storm

*šnꜥ* storm cloud

*šnꜥ* magazine, storehouse

*šnꜥ* repel, deter, turn back, detain, hold back, police

*šnꜥw* policing

*šnw* illness, disease, troubles, need

*šnw* enquiry

*šnw* hair

*šnwt* granary

*šnbt* breast

*šns* cake, loaf

*šnsw* offering stone

*šnš* tear up

*šnt* 100

*šnt, šnṯ* resent, feel hostility toward

*šnt* anger, dispute

*šnt ẖt [r] [n]* vent anger [on]

*šnty* heron

***šnṯ*** sheriff

***šnṯ*** revile

***šnty*** foe

***šnṯw*** fighting

***šndyt*** apron

***šndt, šnḏt*** acacia tree

**šr** ***šr*** stop up, close

***šrr*** be small, junior, short

***šri*** lad, boy, child, younger son

***šrš*** hurry

***šrt*** nose, nostril

***šrt*** a grain

**šḫ** ***šḫm ir(y) f*** potentate

**šs** ***šs*** cord, rope

***šs*** alabaster

***šs*** alabaster vessel

***šsr, šs*** corn

***šsꜣ*** be skilled, wise, know, conversant

***šsꜣw*** prescription

***šsꜣw*** hartebeest

***šsi*** to refine (ore)

***šsp*** receive, accept, take, catch

***šsp, sšp*** daylight, white, dawn

***šsp*** palm (length), 1/7 cubit

***šsp*** image, statue, sphinx

***šspw*** sphinx

***šspt*** room, chamber, chapel

***šspt*** cucumber

***šspt-dḫm*** chorus

***šsm*** leather roll

***šsmt*** malachite

***tꜣ šsmt*** a region east of Egypt

***šsmtt*** (goddess) Shesmetet

***šsr*** arrow

***šsr*** recount, announce

***sšr*** linen

***sšrw*** linen (cloth) bag

***sšr, šs*** thing, concern, action

***mỉ šs*** in good condition

***šsr, šs*** corn

***šst*** alabaster

***št*** ***št*** 100

***št*** (tax) assessment

***štꜣ*** mysterious, difficult, secret

***štꜣw*** secrets

***štꜣt*** secrets

***štyw*** turtle

***štyw*** an offering loaf

***štyt*** sanctuary of god Sokar

***štb*** rebellion

***štm*** be insolent, abuse

***štm*** abuse (someone)

***šṯ*** ***šṯyt*** sanctuary of god Sokar

***šd*** ***šd*** artificial lake

***šdi*** to draw forth, rescue, educate, dig, dig out

 ***šdi*** recite, read out loud

 ***šdi*** suckle, educate

 ***šdy*** ditch

 ***šdyt*** mound

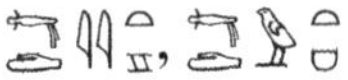 ***šdyt*** pool, plot of land

 ***šdyt*** rubble

 ***šdw*** water skin, cushion, mat

 ***šdw*** waterfowl

 ***šdw, šdwt*** plot of ground

 ***šd-ḥrw*** disturbance

 ***šd-r*** public proclamation

 ***šdt*** Medinet el Fayyum, Crocodilopolis

# ḳ

*ḳꜣ* *ḳꜣꜣ, ḳꜣy, ḳꜣw* hill, height , ascent, high place

*ḳꜣi* be high, tall, loud, exalted

*ḳꜣ ib* haughty

*ḳꜣw* height

*ḳꜣt* height

*ḳꜣyt* high ground, arable land

*ḳꜣyt* high throne

*ḳꜣꜥ* spew out

*ḳꜣw* grains

*ḳ(ꜣ)b* to double

*ḳꜣb* intestine, interior, middle

*ḳꜣbw* winding (of river)

*ḳ(ꜣ)b* to double back

*ḳꜣḥ* earth, plaster

*sḳꜣḥ* to plaster

*ḳrḏn* axe

*ḳꜣs* to bind, string

*ḳꜣḳꜣw* boat, ship

*ḳꜣt* foes

*ḳi* *ḳi* form, image

*mi ḳi f* entire

*ḳis* city of Cusae (UE)

*ḳꜥ* *ḳꜥ* spew out

*ḳꜥḥ* bend the arm, elbow

*ḳꜥḥ* angle, corner

*ḳꜥḥw* sunrise

*ḳꜥḥt* district

***ḳw*** *ḳw* loaf, cake

***ḳb*** *ḳb* scatter

*ḳby* beer jar

*ḳbb* be cool

*sḳbb* to cool or refresh oneself

*ḳbḥ* fountain

*ḳbḥ* death

*ḳbḥ* libate, libation, pour out

*ḳbḥw* libation

*ḳbḥ* Kebh (region of the First Cataract)

*ḳbḥw* sky

*ḳbḥw* marsh birds, wild fowl

*ḳbḥ-snw-f* a son of Horus

*ḳbḥt, ḳbḥw* libation vase

***ḳf*** *ḳfn* bake

*ḳfn* baked goods (cake or biscuit)

***ḳm*** *ḳmꜣ* throw

*ḳmꜣ* create, nature, form

*ḳmꜣw* a type of soldier

*ḳmi* apply resin or gum to

*ḳmi spt* reluctant

*ḳmyt* gum, resin

*ḳmḥ* a loaf

*ḳmd* devise

**ḳn** — *ḳn* offence

*ḳni* be strong, prevail over, strong man, strong, dutiful, brave

- *ḳn* brave man
- *ḳnn* superiority
- *ḳnt* valor, strength, bravery
- *sḳni* strengthen
- *ḳnḳn* beat

*ḳn* be complete, complete

*ḳn* mat

*ḳni* embrace

- *ḳniw* litter, carrying chair

*ḳni* sheaf, bundle

*ḳnbt* corner, angle

*ḳnbt* court of magistrates

*ḳnbty* magistrate

*ḳns* bury

*ḳnd* be furious, angry

**ḳr** — *ḳri* cloud, storm

*ḳrr* frog

*ḳrrt* cave, cavern

*ḳrḥt* vessel

*ḳrḥt* local god, ancestral spirit

*ḳrs* bury, burial

- *ḳrsw* coffin
- *ḳrst* burial
- *ḳrstt* burial equipment

*ḳ(ꜣ)rt* door bolt

ḳḥ ⟨glyphs⟩ ḳḥ jar

ḳs ⟨glyphs⟩, ⟨glyphs⟩ ḳꜣs to bind, string

⟨glyphs⟩ ḳs bone, harpoon

⟨glyphs⟩, ⟨glyphs⟩ ḳsn be irksome, difficult

ḳd ⟨glyphs⟩ ḳd go round

⟨glyphs⟩ mw-pf-ḳdw the Euphrates River

⟨glyphs⟩ ḳd character, form, nature

⟨glyphs⟩, ⟨glyphs⟩, ⟨glyphs⟩, ⟨glyphs⟩, ⟨glyphs⟩ ḳd build, fashion (pots), form

⟨glyphs⟩, ⟨glyphs⟩ ḳd builder

⟨glyphs⟩ sḳd cause to build

⟨glyphs⟩ ḳdw enemies from Kode

⟨glyphs⟩ ḳdwt drawings

⟨glyphs⟩ ḳdtt a Syrian tree

⟨glyphs⟩, ⟨glyphs⟩, ⟨glyphs⟩, ⟨glyphs⟩ ḳd(d) to sleep, slumber

⟨glyphs⟩ ḳddw slumber

⟨glyphs⟩ nḳdd sleep

⟨glyphs⟩ sḳdd cause to sleep, let sleep

⟨glyphs⟩ ḳdt 1/10 "**deben**" (about 1/3 oz.)

# k

*k* you (masc)

*k* I, me, my

**kꜣ** *kꜣ* soul, personality, mood, attribute, fortune, will (of king)

*n kꜣ n* for the *kꜣ* of

*ḥm-kꜣ* ka priest

*kꜣ* bull, ox

*kꜣ nḫt* strong bull, victorious bull (title for pharaoh)

*kꜣ n idr* best bull (of the herd)

*kꜣ* so, then

*kꜣi* think about, plan, so, then

*kꜣt* thought, plan, device, plot

*kꜣw* food

*kꜣw* food, essence

*kꜣp* fumigate, burn incense

*kꜣp* harim, nursery

*kꜣp [m]* to cover [with], hide

*kꜣpw* roof

*kꜣpt* linen cover

*kꜣmw* vinyard, orchard

*kꜣmw* vintner

*kꜣnw* garden

*kꜣny, kꜣry* gardener, vintner

*kꜣr(i)* chapel, shrine

*kꜣhs* be harsh, overbearing

*kꜣš* Kush (Nubia)

*kꜣ-ḥr-kꜣ* fifth month festival

***kꜣt*** plan, thought, device

***kꜣt*** work, construction

***ẖrp kꜣt*** controller of works

***kỉ*** — ***kỉ [ḥr]*** cry out loud, complain [about]

***ky*** — ***ky*** monkey

***ky, kt, kywy*** other, another

***kt ẖt*** others

***kw*** — ***kwỉ*** I, me, my

***kw(i)*** other, another

***kb*** — ***kbnt*** ship

***kp*** — ***kpn(y)*** Byblus (in Phoenicia)

***kf*** — ***kf*** uncover, unclothe, strip, deprive, gather, despoil

***kf ḥr*** to plunder

***kfꜣ*** rear (of bird), bottom (of a pot)

***kfꜣ-ib*** be discreet, trustworthy, careful

***kfꜣ-ib [ḥr]*** trustworthy [in]

***m-kf(ꜣ)t*** "indeed"

***kfꜥ*** capture

***kfꜥ*** shoot at

***kfꜥw*** warrior

***kftiw*** type of ship

***kftiw*** Crete

***km*** — ***km*** be complete, completion, success

***km*** black

***kmy(t)*** herd (of cattle)

***km wr*** the Bitter Lakes (East of Egypt) (lit - the Great Black) *kmt* Egypt (the Black Land)

*kmt* a jar

***kn*** *kni* be sullen

*knʿnw* Canaanites

*knmtyw* those who dwell in darkness

*knḥ* dark

*kns* pubic region, vagina

***kr*** *krr* Gerar (in Syria)

***ks*** *ksi* to bow down

*ksw* bowing down, crouching

*ksm* thwart, treat defiantly

***kš*** *kš* Kush (Nubia)

***kk*** *kk* be dark

*kkw* darkness

***kt*** *kt* pettiness

*kt* other, another

*kt ḫt* others

*kit* shout of acclaim

*ktwt* cauldrons

*ktkt* quiver

*ktt* be small, trifling, little one

# g

**g3** — *g3w* be narrow, constricted, lack (something), short (of breath), deprive (of breath)

*g3wt* bundles, tribute, dues

**gy** — *gy* an offering loaf

**gw** — *gw3* tighten, besiege, be choked

*gw3w3* fetter, bind fast, throttle, choke

*gw3t* (storage) chest

*gwg* shout

**gb** — *gb, gbb* (earth god) Geb

*gb3* arm

*gb3* side (of room)

*gb(b)* the white fronted "**Geb**" goose

*gbgb* be lame, fell (an enemy)

*gbgbyt* fall headlong, prostate

*gbtyw* Coptus (UE)

**gf** — *gf* monkey

*gfn, gnf* to rebuff

**gm** — *gmi* find

*gmw* mourning

*gm wš* found defective, destroyed

*gmḥ* look at

*sgmḥ* cause to see, glimpse

*gmḥsw* hawk

*gmḥt* wick

*gmḥt* braded hair

*gmgm* break up, break

*gmt* black ibis

**gn** *gn* (bowl) stand

*gnwt* annals, records

*gnwty* sculptor

*gnbtw* foreigners from Punt

*gnf* to rebuff

*gnn* be soft, weak

*sgnn* soften, weaken

*gnẖ* serve

*gnẖt* star

**gr** *gr* be silent, quiet, still, silence, cease, desist

*i(w)grt* necropolis

*grw* silent one

*grt, gr* moreover, now, further, either

*grḥ* cease, finish

*sgrḥ* pacify, make peaceful

*grḥ* night

*grg* to snare, found, establish

*grg* falsehood, lie

*grgy* liar

*grt* moreover, now, further, either

**gḥ** *gḥ, gḥs* gazelle

**gs** *gs* anoint

*gs* side, half, border, lay low (an enemy)

*r gs, ḥr gs* beside, in the presence of

*gs(wy) fy* its two sides

*gs-pr* administrative district

*gs-ḥry* top, uppermost

*rdi ḥr gs* partial, bias, dispose of, kill

*gs [m]* anoint [with]

*gsꜣ* tilt, favor

*gsꜣ* favorite

*gsi* to run

*gst* speed

*gsy* Kus (UE)

*gsw* neighbors

*gsw* half-loaves

*gsty* palette

*gg* — *ggwy, ggwt [ḥr]* dazzled, amazement, stare [at]

*ggt* kidney

*gt* — *gtḥ* be tired

## t (often replaced by ṯ )

- -*t* ( infinitive - suffix)
- -*t* you (fem), feminine (suffix)
- *it* father
  - *it.f* his father
- *t* bread
  - *t ḥḏ* white bread

**tꜣ**

- *tꜣ* this, the, she of
- *tꜣ* land, earth
  - *wpt tꜣ* earth's beginning, the extreme south
  - *ḥry-tꜣ* survivor
  - *tꜣw* lands (as opposed to deserts), countries
  - *tꜣwy* the two lands, Egypt
  - *tꜣ-wr* larboard, west bank
  - *tꜣ wr* nome of Abydos and This
  - *tꜣ mri* Egypt
  - *tꜣ mḥw* Lower Egypt, the Delta, Lower Egyptian
  - *tꜣ-nḥs(y)* Nubia
  - *tꜣ nṯr* vassal state (lit - god's land)
  - *tꜣ-st(i)* Nubia
  - *tꜣ š* the Fayyum (lit - lake land)
  - *tꜣ šsmt* a region east of Egypt
  - *tꜣ-tmw* all men
  - *tꜣ ṯnn* (earth god) Tatjenen
  - *tꜣ ḏsr* necropolis
  - *tpyw-tꜣ* the living (lit - those upon the earth)

*dhn tꜣ* touch forehead to ground

*tꜣ* kiln

*tꜣ* be hot, cook

*tꜣy i* my

, , , , , (×)(), *tꜣš* boundary, frontier

, , *tꜣ, tꜣyt* curtain, shroud

*tꜣyty* he of the curtain, shrouded one

*tꜣ-wr* larboard

*ti* *ti* "May she have"

, *ti* lo, behold, now

*hr ti* you are content

*ti* Ty (in Syria)

*tiw* Yes!

, *tisw* stick, staff

, , , *ti šps* a tree, a spice

, *tit* "**tyet**" amulet

*tit* pestle

, , () *tit* figure, image, shape, design

()()()()() *titi* crush, trample down

*ty* - *-ty* (fem. dual suffix) very, two, pair of

, *ty* "pray tell", "forsooth", "I suppose"

*tyntꜥ* Tineta (water channel in Nubia)

*tw* *tw* one, someone, this, that, these, those

*tw* you, your

*twꜣ* claim

*twꜣ* poor man, inferior

, *twꜣ* to support, lean

*twr [ḥr]* show respect [for]

*twr* reed

*twri* be pure

*twt* statue. image, figure

*stwt* resemble, even out, praise

*twt* pleasing, fair, fitting, like

*tb* *ṯbt* sandal

*tbtb* hoist

*tp* *tp* head, chief, tip, beginning (of time), upon

*rs tp* vigilant

*tp* (number of) persons (lit - heads)

*tp-iꜣt* due time (to act)

*tpy* chief, principal, first, who or which is upon

*tpy* chief, first, first month, who or which is upon

*tp-ꜥw(y)* who are in front, before, ancestors, former

*tpyw-tꜣ* the living (lit - those upon the earth)

*tp-ꜥ* before, (into) the presence of

*tp-wꜣt* journey, beginning (of reign)

*tp-m* in the direction of, in front of

*tp mꜣꜥ* accompanying, escorting

*tp-n-sšmt* specification

*tp-rꜥ-mḏ* 10 day week

*tp(y)-r* utterance

*tp-rnpt* feast of the first of the year

*tp-rd* instructions, rules, principless

*tp-ḥwt* roof

*tp ḥr mꜣst* in mourning (lit - head upon ones lap)

*tp-ḥsb* reckoning, norm, standard, rectitude

*tpt* uraeus

*tp(y)-tȝ* survivor

*tpt-ꜥ* former state

*tpt-r* utterance

*tp-tr* festival of the beginning of the season

*tpt-rd* task

*tpt--ḥr(y)* master

*tpr* sniff, breathe

*tpiw* ox

*tpḥt* cavern, snake hole

*tpt* fine oil

*tf* — *it* father

*tf, tfȝ* that, yonder

*tfy* upon, when

*tfn* orphan

*tfnt* (goddess) Tefenet

*tm* — *itm* (god) Atum

*tm* be complete, perfect, closed, everything, all creation, entire, throughout

*tm* close (mouth)

*ṯmȝ* mat

*tmw* everyone, all mankind

*tȝ-tmw* all men

*tms* turn (the face)

*tm* not (negates verb)

*tm* (part of the title *ḥry tm*)

*ḥry tm* an obscrue title

*tmꜣ* land survey

*tmꜣyt* mat

*tmm* not having been

*tmhỉ* Temhi land

*tmḥw* Libyan(s)

*tmsw* injury, harm

*tmt* sledge

*tn* — *tn* you, your

*tn* you, this

*tn* where? whence?

*rṯn, rtn* whither

*tni* old, decrepit

*tnỉ [r]* to distinguish, raise up [over]

*stnỉ* raise up, distinguish, honor

*tnw* number, each, every

*r tnw sp* every time that

*tnbḫ* shrink, recoil

*tnm* go astray

*stnm* lead astray

*tnm* beer jug

*t nt* she of

*tr* — *tr* time, season

*tr* "pray tell", "forsooth", "I suppose"

*tri* show respect for

*tryt* respect

**th** — *thi* wander, transgress, disobey, cause to wander
- *thw* transgressor
- *thr* a Syrian warrior

**tḥ** — *tḥnw* Libya
- *tḥnw* Libyans
- *tḥnt* fayence, glass

**tẖ** — *t ḥḏ* white bread
- *tẖ* plumb bob
- *tẖi* be drunk
- *tẖi* drink deep
- *tẖw* drunkard
- *tẖt* drunkedness
- *tẖy* the second month
- *tẖb* immerse, soak
- *tẖn* obelisk
- *tẖtẖ* disorder

**tš** — *tš* spit out
- *tš* smash, grind, split
- *tꜣš* boundary
- *tši [r]* be missing, stray [from]
- *tšw* deserter
- *tšꜣ* smash, crush

**tk** — *tkꜣ* torch, candle
- *tkn* approach, draw near, meet
- *stkn* cause to approach, bring on
- *tks* pierce, penetrate
- *tkk* attack, violate (space)
- *tkkw* attackers

**ṯ** (often replaced by *t* )

*ṯ* you (fem)

*ṯꜣ*

*ṯꜣ* nestling, child

*ṯꜣ* pellet

*ṯꜣyw* pellets

*ṯꜣỉ* take, gird on, rob

*ṯꜣwt* theft

*ṯꜣ-ỉb* able

*ṯꜣy* male, man

*ṯꜣy* bull calf

*ṯꜣw* breath, wind, air

*ṯꜣw* book

*ṯꜣw* take up, seize, rob

*ṯꜣwt* sail

*ṯꜣb* a jar

*ṯꜣbt* loan (of grain)

*ṯꜣm* cloak, swaddling clothes

*ṯꜣm* be veiled

*mṯꜣm* sheer dress

*ṯꜣm* foreskin

*ṯꜣm ḥr m* show indulgence to

*ṯꜣr* fasten, make fast, preserve

*ṯꜣr* cabin

*ṯꜣt(y)* vizer

*ṯỉ*

*ṯỉt* dais

*ṯỉṯỉ* trot

**ṯw**

*ṯw* you, your

**ṯb**

*ṯb(i)* be shod

*ṯbw* sandal maker

*ṯbwt* sandal, sole

*ṯbwty* pair of sandles

*ṯbt* vase

**ṯp**

*ṯpḥt* cavern, snake hole

*ṯmꜣ* land survey

*ṯmꜣꜥ* strong armed

*ṯmḥ, ṯmḥw* Libyan(s)

*ṯms* red

*ṯms* be besmeared

**ṯn**

*ṯn* you, your

*ṯn* you, this

*ṯn* where? whence?

*rṯn* whither

*ṯn(i) [r]* to distinguish, raise up [over]

*sṯni* raise up, distinguish

*ṯni* basin

*ṯni* Thinis

*ṯniꜣ* throw stick

*ṯny* This (UE)

*ṯnw* number, counting, each

*ṯnwt* number, quantity

*ṯnwt* number of cattle

*ṯnwt* number of prisoners

*ṯnwt r* greater amount than

*ṯnf* enjoyment

*ṯnfyt* sail

*ṯnnt* sanctuary at Memphis

*ṯnnt* (goddess) Tjenenet

*ṯnr* eager

*ṯnḥr* hawk

*ṯnt* difference

*ṯntt* raised platform

*ṯntꜣt* canopy, dais

*ṯr* *ṯrp* a type of goose

*ṯrt* willow tree

*ṯḥ* *ṯḥw* rejoice, exultation, joy

*ṯḥn* gleam

*ṯḥn [ḥnꜥ]* draw near (to fight) [with]

*ṯḥnw* Libya

*ṯḥnw* Libyans

*ṯḥnt* fayence, glass

*ṯḥḥ* exult

*ṯḥḥwt* exultation

*ṯs* *ṯs* sandbank

*ṯs* marshal (troops), tie, join, bind, arrange

*ṯs-pri* fighting

*ṯs* saying, utterance

*ṯsw* commander

*ṯsi* raise, lift up, recruit, mount, rise

*ṯsi* go up

*ṯsi m* feel resentment at, blame

*ṯswt* complaints

*ṯswrt* offering loaf

*ṯsm* hound

*ṯst* hill

, *ṯst* ridge, range

*ṯst* knot, vertebra

*ṯst* troop, unit

*ṯt* , *ṯtf* overflow, pour forth, flow down

*ṯṯ* *ṯṯt* one who applies fetters

# d (often replaced by ḏ )

*d(W)* give, place, put, implant, strike

**dꜣ** *dꜣiw* loin cloth

*dꜣb* figs

*dꜣr, dꜣir* subdue

*dꜣt, dwꜣt* netherworld

**di** *di, rdi* to give, place, cause, grant

*rdi ib m-sꜣ* be anxious about

*rdi ib ḫnt* pay attention to

*di(w), dy* gift, gratuity

*di ḥr gs* dispose of, kill, show partiality

*di(w)* provisions

*diwt* set of five

*di ḥr gs* dispose of, kill, show partiality

*di m ib-f* determine

**dy** *dyt, diwt* shriek, cry out, bellow

*dyt, ḏyt* papyrus marsh, papyrus plant

**dw** *dwꜣw* morning, tomorrow, rise early, dawn

*dwꜣ* adore, praise

*dwꜣt* adore, praise

*dwꜣt, dwꜣyt* morning

*dwꜣt* netherworld

*dwꜣ-mut* a son of Horus

*dwn* stretch out

*dws* malign

**db** *db, dib* hippopotamus

*db* horn, wing ( of the army)

*dbi* to stop up, block

*dbn* helmet

*dbn* go around, travel around, encircle, recur

*dbnw* circumference, circuit, circle

*dbnt* circuit (of the ocean)

*dbn* "**deben**" weight, about 3 ounces

*dbḥ* to beg for, request

*dbḥw* requirements, necessities

*dbḥw* measure for offerings

*dbḥt* necessaries

*dbḥt* funerary meal

*dbḥt-ḥtp* altar

*ḏbt* brick

**dp** *dp* to taste, experience

*dp* taste

*dp* part of Buto (Delta)

*dpy* crocodile

*dpt* ship, boat

*dpt-nṯr* the divine bark

*dpty* an offering

**dm** *dm* be sharp

*dm* to pierce

*dm* sharpen

*dmt* knife

*dm* pronounce, proclaim (a name), be renowned

*dmꜣ* bind together

*dmꜣ* cut off (heads)

*dmꜣw* groups

*dmꜣt* wing

*dmỉ* fruit dish

*dmỉ* touch, arrive at, accrue

*sdmỉ* attach, annex

*dmỉ* town, abode

*ỉdmỉ* red linen

*dmḏ* unite, entire, total, reassemble, bring together, accumulate

*dmḏyt* festival cycle

**dn**

*dn* chop off

*dnỉ* dam off, restrain, hold back

*dnỉt* dam

*dnỉt* bowl

*dnỉt* a festival

*dnỉw* share, portion

*dnw* flaw

*dnwt* families

*dnḥ* wing

*dns* be heavy, irksome, burdensome

*dns* heaviness

*dns ib* reluctant (lit - heavy heart)

*dnsw* weights

**dr**

*dr* remove, quell, drive out, subdue, expel, repress

*drp* offer food (to), feed (someone)

*drpw* offerings

*ḏrf* writing

*ḏrt, ḏꜣt* hand, trunk (of elephant), handle (of jar), recite

*ḏrt* hand

***dh***

*dhn [r]* promote [to] (position)

*dhnt* forehead

*dhn tꜣ* touch the forehead to the ground

***dḥ***

*dḥꜣ* straw

*dḥi* be low, lowly, hang down

*sdḥ* bring down,, humiliate

*dḥr* bitter, sour

*dḥrt* bitterness, sickness

*dḥr(i)* skin, hide, leather

*dḥty* lead

***ds***

*ds* flint

*ds* knife

*ds* beer jug, "**des**" (measure)

***dš***

*dšr* red

*dšr* flamingo

*dšrt* the Red Land, desert

*dšrt* red pot

*dšrt* red crown

***dḳ***

*dḳ* flour, powder

*dḳr* press, move, expel

*dḳr(w)* fruit

*dḳ(r)* fruit

***dg***

*dgꜣ* to walk

 ***dgỉ*** to hide, conceal

 ***sdgȝ [r]*** hide or conceal [from]

 ***dgỉ*** to look

***dt*** 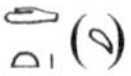 ***ḏrt*** hand, (elephant) trunk, (jar) handle

***dd***  ***ddw, ḏdw*** Busiris (Delta)

 ***ddwn*** a Nubian god

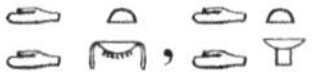 ***ddt*** dish

# ḏ (often replaced by *d* )

***ḏꜣ***   ***ḏꜣ*** fire drill

***ḏꜣ*** stretch forth, extend, reach out, take, eat, provide

***ḏꜣi*** to cross, ferry across

***ḏꜣi*** sail across the sky

***ḏꜣis*** argument, dispute, to contend, argue, oppose

***ḏꜣisw*** disputant

***ḏꜣyt*** transgression, wrong

***ḏꜣytyw*** opponents

***sḏꜣy ḥr*** divert oneself, amuse oneself

***ḏꜣw*** night

***wḏꜣ*** remainder

***ḏꜣf*** fire, burn

***r ḏꜣwt*** in return for, because of

***ḏꜣmw*** young men, troops

***ḏꜣrw*** need, requirement

***ḏꜣrw*** needs, requirements

***ḏꜣhy*** part of Phoenicia and Canaan

***ḏꜣt*** transgression, wrong

***r ḏꜣwt*** in return for, because of

***ḏꜣyt*** transgression, wrongdoing

***ḏꜣytyw*** opponents

***ḏꜣt*** remainder, balance, deficiency

***ḏrt, ḏꜣt*** hand, recite

***ḏꜣtt*** estate

***ns pr n ḏꜣtt*** steward of the estate

*ḏꜣdw* audience hall, hall of columns

*ḏꜣḏꜣ* head (of a group)

*ḏꜣḏꜣ w* pot

*ḏꜣḏꜣt* magistrates, assessors, counsel

*ḏꜣḏꜣt* harp

***ḏy*** *dyt, ḏyt* papyrus marsh, papyrus plant

***ḏꜥ*** *ḏꜥ* to spear, harpoon

*ḏꜥ* type of bread

*ḏꜥbt* charcoal

*ḏꜥ(w)* storm

*ḏꜥm* **"djam"** scepter

*ḏꜥm, ḏꜥmw* fine gold, electrum

*ḏꜥr, ḏꜥ* search out, seek

***ḏw*** *ḏw* mountain

*ḏww* mountains

*ḏw* be bad, evil, sad

*ḏwt* evil, sadness

*ḏws* malign

*ḏwỉ* call

***ḏb*** *ḏbꜣ* Edfu (UE)

*ḏbꜣ* (god's) garment

*ḏbꜣ* stop up, block

*ḏbꜣ* clothe, adorn, repay, block

*ḏbꜣ* replace

*r ḏbꜣ* instead of

*ḏbꜣ-* payment, bribe, repayment, replace

***ḏbꜣw*** payments, rewards, bribes

***ḏbꜣw*** altars

***ḏbꜣt*** dressing room, sarcophagus

***ḏbꜥ*** finger, toe, finger width (1/28 cubit)

***ḏbꜥw t, ḏbꜥt*** signet ring

***ḏbꜥw*** reproach (lit - finger pointing)

***ḏbꜥ [m]*** point the finger [at]

***ḏbꜥ*** 10,000

***ḏbꜥw t, ḏbꜥt*** signet ring

***ḏbw*** pole (of chariot)

***ḏbt*** brick

***ḏf***

***ḏf(ꜣ)w*** provisions

***ḥtpt ḏf(ꜣ)*** food offerings

***sḏfꜣy*** endow, provide for

***ḏfḏ*** pupil of the eye

***ḏn***

***ḏnb*** a offering loaf

***ḏnḥ*** wing

***ḏns*** heavy, irksome, burdensome

***ḏnd*** rage

***ḏr***

***ḏr*** wall, enclosure

***ḏri*** wall

***ḏrit*** wall

***ḏri*** be hard, firm, stoutly

***ḏrit*** wall

***ḏr*** since, end

***r-ḏr-f*** entire

*ḏr ꜥ(wy)* originally, long ago, end, limit

*ḏr ꜥ r* down until

*ḏrw* end, limit

*ḏr ntt* since, because

*ḏrtyw* ancestors

*ḏrw* side

*ḏrw* boundary, limit

*ḏrwy* color, paint

*ḏrwt* hall

*ḏrt, ḏꜣt* hand, (elephant) trunk, (jar) handle

*ḏrt, ḏꜣt* hand, recite

*ḏrt* hand

*ḏrtyw* ancestors

*ḏrḏ* tree leaf

*ḏrḏri* foreigner, foreign

*ḏḥ* *ḏḥwty* (god) Thoth

*ḏḥwtt* festival of Thoth

*ḏḥrw* leather lacings

*ḏs* *ḏs* one's self, one's own

*ḏsr* holy, splendid, private, clear (a road)

*tꜣ ḏsr* necropolis

*ḏsrw* seclusion, privacy, sanctity

*ḏsrw* holy place

*ḏsr-ḏsrw* temple at Deir el Bahri (lit - Holy of Holies)

*ḏsr-imntt* Medinet Habu (lit - Western Holy Place)

*ḏsr ḥpwt* direct the boat, sail

***ḏt*** — *ḏt* cobra

*ḏt* papyrus stem

*ḏt* body, self

*ỉp ḏt. f* grow up (id) (lit - count his self)

*n ḏt. f* his own

*ḏt* eternity, forever

*ḏt* stability, duration

*ḏt* estate, serf

*ḏt* serfs

***ḏd*** — *ḏd* stable, enduring

*sḏd* make permanent

*ḏd* "**djed**" pillar

*ḏd* say, speak, recite, think

*r ḏd* saying that

*ḏd mdw ỉn* speech by, words spoken by

*ḏd mdw* recitation, speech (continued)

*ḏdꜣ* fat

*ḏdỉ* be stable, enduring

*ḏdw* Busiris (LE)

*ḏdb* string, incite

*ḏdft* snake

*ḏdh* imprison

*ḏdḥ* imprison, shut away

*ḏdkw* channel, canal (perhaps the name of same)

*ḏdwt* Mendes (Delta)

Made in the USA
Las Vegas, NV
19 January 2021

16183375R00105